HOW TO BUILD WOODEN BOATS

With 16 Small-Boat Designs

Edwin Monk

DOVER PUBLICATIONS, INC.
New York

TO THE YACHTSMAN
WHO BUILDS HIS OWN BOAT

NOTE

This is an unabridged reprint of a work first published in 1934 that contained some specific information on names, addresses, materials and tools not currently useful. Minor corrections and deletions have been made. Note especially that asbestos is now regarded as hazardous and substitutes should be used.

This Dover edition, first published in 1992, is an unabridged republication of the work originally published in 1934 by Charles Scribner's Sons, New York, under the title, *Small Boat Building for the Amateur, with Sixteen Modern Small Boat Designs, Rowboats, Sailboats, Outboards, a 125-Class Hydroplane and a Runabout*. The text has been reset for this edition and the illustrations have been moved from their original locations.

Manufactured in the United States of America
Dover Publications, Inc., 31 East 2nd Street, Mineola, N.Y. 11501

Library of Congress Cataloging-in-Publication Data

Monk, Edwin.
    How to build wooden boats : with 16 small-boat designs / Edwin Monk.
        p.   cm.
    Rev. ed. of: Small boat building. 1934.
    ISBN 0-486-27313-X
    1. Boatbuilding.   I. Monk, Edwin.   Small boat building.   II. Title.
    VM321.M6   1992
    623.8′202—dc20   92-20138
                                                                          CIP

Contents

Chapter I

General Discussion

THERE IS A certain fascination about boatbuilding, in watching a boat gradually take shape, and this particularly so when the results are through your own efforts. I often wonder if the amateur builder does not derive as much pleasure in the construction of his craft as he does in the use of it. It is at any rate a good hobby or pastime, and the man who builds his boat doubtless gets a bigger "kick" out of boating or yachting than does his brother who pays someone to build it for him.

It is the purpose of this book to present to the amateur boatbuilder a wide variety of small-boat designs and a clear explanation of small-boat construction in general, with particular reference to the designs herein. There is a much better opportunity to explain construction methods and detail in a book of this sort than in magazine designs, where space is limited and construction methods are repeated with each design. Many of the published "how to builds" are excellent, and the methods described and illustrated here are applicable to all of them. These methods and details are not impractical or devised by a novice, but are backed by extensive first-hand experience in small-boat construction and design, and many of these methods are in every-day use in the boat yards of today.

In the plans herein the purpose has been to produce a nice-appearing design that in every way looks the part, but with simplicity of construction always kept in mind. No attempt has been made to cover such subjects as rules of the road, seamanship, etc., and many other things sometimes included in a book of this sort. Some of these are useful, but can be found in other sources.*

Building from Other Plans

Probably the best procedure would be to select as a guide some design shown here that closely resembles the construction of the boat in mind. If the boat is best erected upside down, a set-up line will have to be established, as it is seldom shown on other plans. This is, however, a simple matter and probably the only conversion necessary.

The Round-Bottom Boat

This construction is considered a bit difficult for the amateur, although the professional boatbuilder generally considers the round-bottom construction as easier. This book is not primarily intended to cover this type of boat, but can be of much help, and a separate heading in last part of the text will show its applicability. The clinker or lap-strake boat had best be left to the professional small-boat builder.

Chapman Piloting, Seamanship, and Small Boat Handling is recommended.

Chapter II

Materials

Boatbuilding Woods

EACH LOCALITY HAS its own boatbuilding woods, the choice of which is governed somewhat by proximity of supply. Oak is probably the only wood universally obtainable for small-boat construction. For this reason the builder should be allowed a great deal of latitude in his selection of materials, and to aid him in this as many timber varieties as possible have been touched in the following specification. In the accompanying plans a certain species has been specified for each particular place or member, but this is intended merely as a guide. Boat lumber may be roughly divided into two classifications, which are: framing lumber, including that suitable for keel and stem; and planking lumber, which should include gunwales, stringers, and clamps.

To be suitable for framing its first requirement, aside from strength, is ability to hold fastenings. Therefore it should possess a certain hardness and closeness of grain. As it is generally in narrow widths a tendency to twist or warp is not a serious defect. As small boats are well ventilated, having very few dead-air spaces in them, there is little danger of dry rot, provided a boat is given a reasonable amount of care.

For planking purposes the lumber should bend easily and stay put after fastening; that is, it should not have a tendency to warp or to curl up at the edges. For this reason vertical grain is always ordered for the top sides at least. Hardness or ability to hold fastenings is not required, as all fastenings are through fastenings.

Weight is often quite a factor in the choice of materials, particularly so if the boat is to be a racing hydroplane or outboard, and for purposes of comparison the weight per cubic foot of most boat woods is given in the following table:

Species	Dry	Wet
	POUNDS	POUNDS
Ash	40	49
Birch	32	57
Butternut	35	45
Cedar, Western red	24	41
" Oregon or Port Orford	31	39
" white	22	41
" Spanish	35	42
" Alaska	31	39
Cypress	31	..

Species	Dry	Wet
	POUNDS	POUNDS
Elm	45	48
Douglas fir or Oregon pine	32	40
Hackmatack	35	..
Hickory	48	..
Locust	46	66
Honduras mahogany	44	50
Philippine mahogany	39	..
Maple	43	46
Oak, white	46	62
White pine	26	39
Oregon pine	32	40
Yellow pine	44	47
Spruce	27	38
Teak	48	58

The following is a general classification of boat woods as to purpose for which they are used in small-boat construction.

Keel.—Oak, mahogany, Douglas fir, yellow pine, teak, and Alaska cedar.

Stem.—Generally of hardwood, oak, mahogany, teak, and bagac.

Planking.—The cedars, white, Port Orford, Alaska and Western red; also cypress, mahogany and its sister wood, Spanish cedar; white pine, which is largely used for dories, and Western spruce. Teak is sometimes used, and aside from its weight is of course splendid.

All planking should be practically clear, also vertical grain if possible, particularly for the top sides where also wide planks should be avoided (except for skiffs and similar construction).

Framing.—Oak and mahogany are most widely used, but where lightness is a large factor spruce and the harder cedars also, as well as close-grained Douglas fir. These softer woods may be used in any sawed frame boat, but larger fastenings should compensate for the poorer holding power. Material for sawed-frames need not be clear, as knots (if not too many) may be easily avoided and a much cheaper grade of lumber used. Use bending oaks for bent frames.

Transom.—Being wide, it has a tendency to warp, which is one objection to oak; nevertheless oak should be included with mahogany, teak, and Spanish cedar. Among the soft woods the harder cedars, spruce, and Douglas fir; these should be vertical grain if possible.

Gunwales.—Any of the planking woods will do, but as subject to hard usage, oak or mahogany are better.

Seam Battens, Bilge Stringers, and Seat Risers.—Same as planking, but to include oak and yellow pine.

Seats and Floor Boards.—Generally are of soft woods, as lightness and weather resistance are most required. The cedars, spruce, Douglas fir, cypress, and white and yellow pine are used though mahogany and Spanish cedar are ideal. The navy often uses ash thwarts or seats.

Decking.—If canvas covered is always tongue-and-groove or matched and of cedar or white pine. If it is to be caulked, mahogany, teak, and Spanish cedar are generally used. Caulked decking should not be wider than 2½″ and tongue-and-groove for canvas deck 3″.

Deck Beams.—Douglas fir and yellow pine are commonly used; also oak and mahogany. Spruce is often chosen for its light weight, but does not hold deck fastenings well.

Cabin Trunks.—Mahogany, Spanish cedar, and teak are probably the most satisfactory if the trunk is to be varnished, in which case the whole exterior trim should be to match; any of the cedars are very good if to be painted.

Guards.—Oak, mahogany, bagac, and sometimes teak or almost any hardwood.

Masts and Spars.—Spruce is said to be the strongest wood for its weight in the Western Hemisphere and is almost universally used. Douglas fir, though excellent, is heavier.

Breast Hooks and Knees.—Oak, mahogany, or almost any hardwood.

Plywood.—Something should be said about plywood and the several patented composition boards. They are ideal for bulkheads, web frames, and stiffeners, and several stock-boat manufacturers are using them for planking in certain types of boats. The plywood must be put together with waterproof glue, otherwise it is absolutely useless. It should be well painted, especially the edges. Make sure that any of the above materials are guaranteed for the purpose by the manufacturer.

The Lumber Order

Most of the cedars and also the hardwoods are stocked in the rough and surfaced to order. Generally one quarter of an inch is allowed for surfacing two sides, but this depends on how closely the lumber has been sawed. It is sometimes possible to get ¹⁵/₁₆″ boards from 1″ stock and it should not be necessary to lose more than ⅛″ in the surfacing process.

Plank Thickness		Plank Widths	
ROUGH	FINISHED	ROUGH	FINISHED
1″	¹¹/₁₆″	2″	1⅝″
1″	²⁵/₃₂″	3″	2⅝″
1¼″	1¹/₁₆″	4″	3⅝″
1½″	1⁵/₁₆″	6″	5⅝″
2″	1⅝″	8″	7½″
2½″	2⅛″	10″	9½″
3″	2⅝″	12″	11½″
3½″	3⅛″	and so forth	
4″	3⅝″		

By this I mean that a ⅞″ board surfaced on both sides should be obtained from 1″ stock.

Douglas fir and several of the pines may be purchased and, in fact, are most frequently sold surfaced four sides or S. 4 S. Following are the standard Douglas fir or Oregon pine sizes and the rough stock they are each made from.

In ordering a 2 × 6 from the above you will, for example, receive a piece 1⅝″ × 5⅝″ unless you order net sizes, in which case you will get the exact size ordered. It is always cheaper to use stock materials, and the above sizes should be kept in mind when making out the lumber order. When ordering, include something for crossbands and other odds and ends used in setting up the boat.

Some explanation should be made of the lumber orders accompanying each of the plans in this book. The thickness is always net, but the width may be either net or the surfaced dimensions unless followed by the letter N. For example, if the order calls for one Pc. ¾″ × 10″, either ¾″ × 9½″ or ¾″ × 10″ will do. In case you can obtain planking or framing lumber S. 2 S. or S. 4 S. always choose the former as even this slight extra width may be useful. Following are some symbols used by the lumberman. S. 2 S. means surfaced two sides, S. 1 S. 1 E. is surfaced one side and one edge and so on, N. means net or exact size ordered, V. G. means vertical grain, B. M. means board measure.

Air-seasoned lumber is in every way superior to kiln-dried; particularly is this true of planking. With a little forethought the builder can often season the planking himself. Quite a bit of time usually elapses before he is ready to use it, and if piled with slats between or stuck and placed where air will circulate through the pile, it will soon dry out.

Fastenings

For boatbuilding purposes all fastenings must be either galvanized or of some corrosion-resisting metal, such as copper, brass, or bronze.

Nails

Nails are generally galvanized unless they are to be clinched or riveted, in which case they are copper. The square, cut, or boat nail is used for plank fastenings (see "Plank Fastenings"). The round or wire nail is used elsewhere about the boat and its rough, galvanized surface adds greatly to its holding power. In the dory lap, seam battens, or wherever a clinched fastening is required, the copper cut or boat nail is used. They should be driven against a hold-on as in Fig. 18, and not bent over after driving. Wire nails are ordered by "penny," boat nails by length, and the first table on page 4 shows lengths per "penny" and approximate number of nails to the pound.

Screws

Brass or composition screws are superior to the galvanized in that the threads are much sharper and clear cut. The screw must be galvanized after the thread is cut, and the zinc coating tends to fill in between the threads and destroys the clear-cut edges. Brass or bronze screws for this reason are always used for the smaller sizes, but from a

NUMBER IN POUND				
Penny	Length in Inches	Galv. Boat	Galv. Wire	Copper Boat
	¾	500	800	800
	⅞	450	700	600
2.............	1	400	550	495
3.............	1¼	300	400	320
4.............	1½	200	260	215
5.............	1¾	135	170	155
6.............	2	95	110	115
7.............	2¼	68	80	85
8.............	2½	50	70	65
10.............	3	33	57	44
12.............	3¼	28	50	37
16.............	3½	24	43	30
20.............	4	20	30	20

SCREW SIZES IN INCHES					
Size No.	Dia. of Shank	Dia. of Head	Size No.	Dia. of Shank	Dia. of Head
4	.109" or ⅛"−	¼"	14	.241" or ¼"−	½"
6	.135" or 9/64"−	5/16"	16	.268" or 9/32"−	9/16"
8	.162" or 11/64"−	11/32"	18	.293" or 5/16"−	⅝"+
10	.188" or 3/16"	⅜"	24	.374" or ⅜"	¾"
12	.215" or 7/32"	7/16"	28	.427" or 7/16"−	⅞"

Bolts

Carriage bolts have largely replaced the old clinch bolt, and may be purchased in diameters from 3/16" up and in almost any length. If possible, purchase the cut thread and not the pressed thread bolt. As in screw sizes it is often desirous to know the diameter of the head, this is given in the following:

Bolt	Head	Bolt	Head
3/16"	½"	7/16"	1"
¼"	⅝"	½"	1⅛"
5/16"	¾"	9/16"	1¼"
⅜"	⅞"	⅝"	1⅜"

number ten screw up the galvanized one does very well. The following is a useful table of screw sizes. The size of head is given as occasionally when the head is to be counterbored for and plugged, this dimension is of importance. The head is roughly twice the shank diameter.

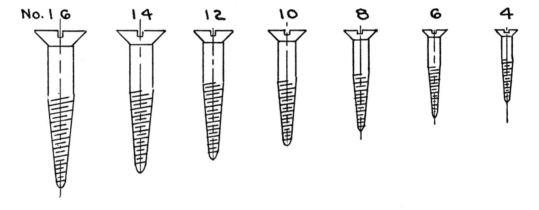

SHOWING ACTUAL SCREW SIZES

4

Chapter III

Assembling

Lofting or "Laying Down"

THIS CONSISTS IN enlarging to full size on the mould loft floor the lines of the boat. These consist of three views of the hull lines (see Fig. No. 1); one viewed from above is called the "half breadth," showing the shape of deck, and of horizontal sections through the hull, called water lines and abbreviated W. L. on the plans. In the lines of a round-bottom boat the diagonals would also be shown, but we are not concerned with them here. This plan is generally at the bottom. Above it is the profile or side view of the boat, showing height of deck or top of sheer strake, rabbet, keel bottom, etc., and often some vertical fore-and-aft sections called "buttocks." The last or body plan is a view from each end of the boat, showing vertical cross-sections of the hull, and as both sides are alike the shape of the forward end is shown one side and the aft end on the other side of a common centreline. In all the above plans the bow is shown to the right. The different lines drawings as designated above are also labelled in plans of *Tern,* an 18′ runabout. Often the body plan is superimposed over the profile, as in many of the plans shown here.

I have endeavored to make it possible, with few exceptions, to construct each boat by laying out the body plan only (see Fig. No. 6), the keel, stem, etc., being shown in separate detail. There is something to be gained, however, in completely lofting almost any boat. A slight unfairness in a scale drawing is greatly magnified when enlarged to full size; these discrepancies can be eliminated in the mould loft and at the same time the amateur will gain valuable experience in the operation. There is no advantage in laying down the simple skiffs or punts, and the builder can follow his own inclination as to the others.

A clean, unpainted or freshly painted surface is the best loft floor, but light-colored building paper will do and has a certain advantage in that the lines may be stowed away for future use. Referring to Fig. No. 1, the first thing is the base line, then the centreline parallel to it, and the frame stations 1, 2, 3, etc., square off base and centreline. The boatbuilder makes one line do for horizontal centre, and base line, and superimposes the three lines drawings one over the other. You can do this if you wish, but try to keep the body plan separate. If possible, and it is not too large, put it on a sort of enlarged drawing board; you can then lift this on to the bench or some horses and assemble your frames there. For clarity, the frame outlines in Fig. No. 1 are shown at their respective stations instead of being all

assembled in a body plan, as in Fig. No. 5, and the station line is in each case used as the vertical centreline. The waterlines are now drawn in on the profile and body plan, and the buttocks on the half-breadth and body plan all are straight lines so far.

All straight lines, including a body-plan centreline, being laid out, we may turn our attention to the offsets. These are applied first to the body plan and each frame is taken separately, the dimensions or offsets applied, and the frame drawn in lightly. To make this clear the offsets of Station No. 3 have been taken as an example. Refer from the offsets to the half-breadth and profile plans and you will see how each is applied (Fig. No. 1; also see Fig. No. 6). If you are laying out the body plan only, this plan (Figs. Nos. 5 and 6) will finish the operation of lofting, and any reference above to profile and half-breadth will be disregarded. The plank thickness must yet be taken off, however, at each frame.

It may seem strange that offsets are not given to inside of planking or actual frame shape instead of to outside of hull. This, however, is standard practice with all naval architects and boatbuilders and for practical reasons. Displacement and all calculations are made to the outside of plank and plank thickness can be deducted with greater accuracy in the mould loft than on small lines drawings; also the rabbet and bearding line would complicate offsets if to inside of plank. On small boats the thickness is simply deducted on the body plan and a new line drawn representing the actual frame, not, however, until the operation of lofting is completed.

Turning now to the fore-and-aft lines, the stem profile is laid out from the dimensions given (or by scaling the plan) and connected with keel bottom. From this point all lines are now obtained from the body plan in the process of fairing up. This consists of taking the half-breadths and heights from the body plan and transferring them to their separate stations on the half-breadth and profile. Take each line separately; for instance, take all the sheer heights and mark them on their respective stations and spring a batten through these spots. Fig. No. 1 shows how the endings of these lines at stem are obtained for the half-breadth plan by squaring them down from stem face on the profile. The sheer height and chine must be run in the profile before these lines can be ended in the half-breadth, and the process is reversed for the buttocks if shown, and if they intersect with chine this is squared up to chine in profile. A thin batten about the size of a yardstick is used in

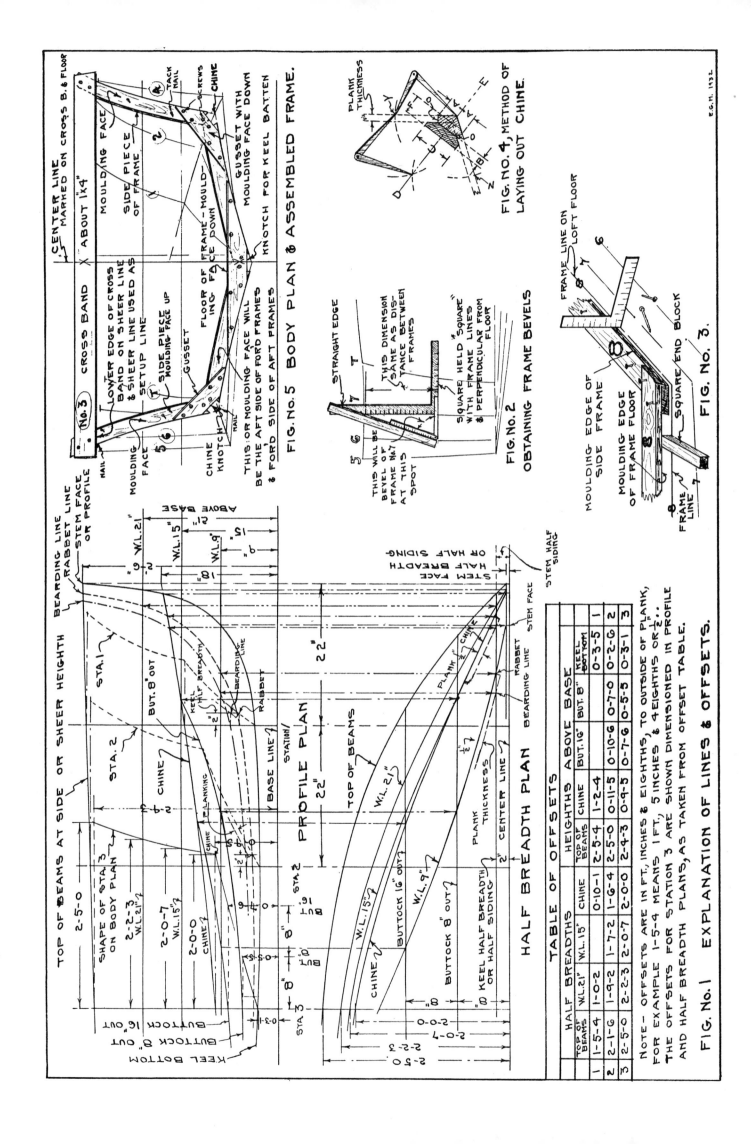

FIG. NO. 3 BODY PLAN & ASSEMBLED FRAME.

FIG. NO. 4, METHOD OF LAYING OUT CHINE.

FIG. NO. 2 OBTAINING FRAME BEVELS

FIG. NO. 3.

HALF BREADTH PLAN

PROFILE PLAN

TABLE OF OFFSETS

	HALF BREADTHS				HEIGHTS ABOVE BASE				
	TOP OF BEAMS	W.L.21"	W.L.15"	CHINE	TOP OF BEAMS	CHINE	BUT.16"	BUT. 8"	KEEL BOTTOM
1	1-5-4	1-0-2		0-10-1	2-5-4	1-2-4			0-3-5	1
2	2-1-6	1-9-2	1-7-2	1-6-4	2-5-0	0-11-5	0-10-6	0-7-0	0-2-6	2
3	2-5-0	2-2-3	2-0-7	2-0-9	2-4-3	0-9-5	0-7-6	0-5-5	0-3-1	3

NOTE — OFFSETS ARE IN FT., INCHES & EIGHTHS, TO OUTSIDE OF PLANK, FOR EXAMPLE 1-5-4 MEANS 1 FT., 5 INCHES & 4 EIGHTHS OR 1½".. THE OFFSETS FOR STATION 3 ARE SHOWN DIMENSIONED IN PROFILE AND HALF BREADTH PLANS, AS TAKEN FROM OFFSET TABLE.

FIG. NO. 1 EXPLANATION OF LINES & OFFSETS.

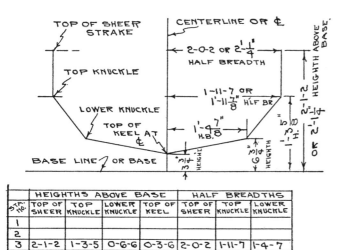

	HEIGHTS ABOVE BASE				HALF BREADTHS		
STA. NO.	TOP OF SHEER	TOP KNUCKLE	LOWER KNUCKLE	TOP OF KEEL	TOP OF SHEER	TOP KNUCKLE	LOWER KNUCKLE
1							
2							
3	2-1-2	1-3-5	0-6-6	0-3-6	2-0-2	1-11-7	1-4-7

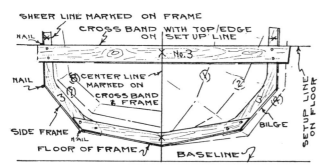

EXPLANATION OF OFFSETS ABOVE, AND
BELOW A FRAME OF ONE OF SMALLER
BOATS READY TO REMOVE FROM FLOOR
FIG. No. 6

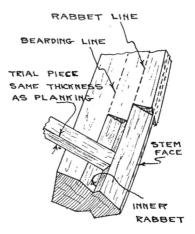

CUTTING RABBET IN
STEM & FOREFOOT
FIG. No. 7

transferring all marks, which are transferred from body plan to stick and thence to the other plans much easier than could be done with a rule. Most of the above may be made clear by a study of Fig. No. 1 much better than it can be explained.

One of the gunwales, clamps, or stringers will make a good batten, but it must be straight and fair; spring it against finish nails driven in at the spots, do not drive nails into batten except when using it on the flat and then just enough to prevent it springing up. For sharp curves use batten on edge and for easy curves, such as sheer and rabbet, place it flat on the floor. It will have to be let out a little here and in a bit there until it forms a fair line (no kinks or bumps), and then marked in. As each line is faired up the body plan is corrected to conform with it, and when all have been run the body plan can be permanently marked in.

In Fig. No. 1, I have tried to show how rabbet and bearding lines are obtained and Figs. Nos. 7, 8, and 11 show just what these lines are. The stem half-siding or half-width is run on half-breadth plan and its intersection with the various waterlines, chine, etc., squared up to these respective lines in the profile, as shown in Fig. No. 1. A thin batten is sprung between the spots and the rabbet line drawn in. The bearding line is obtained by marking off the plank thickness on the waterlines in the half-breadth and squaring its intersection with the stem half-breadth up to profile as for the rabbet line. In Fig. No. 1 at stations 1 and 2 in the profile is shown how rabbet and bearding line are obtained for forefoot from the body plan. This is done by

laying out stem and keel half-siding in body plan, and its point of intersection with each frame line will be the height of rabbet above base at respective stations. Fig. No. 8 further illustrates this process.

This should complete the operation of lofting, and the plank thickness can now be deducted at each frame. Laying out the chine, how to obtain frame bevels, beam camber, etc., are taken up in the order they would be reached in constructing the boat. This brings to mind the advantages of completely lofting the boat; for if carefully done little trimming or fairing up will be needed on frames or rabbet after setting up, and the bevelled side of stem will fair in with the planking exactly.

In the designs shown here the offsets marked keel bottom are heights above base to bottom of keel at centreline and those marked rabbet are heights to rabbet line on side of keel (Fig. No. 8), in which case it is only necessary to connect this line with your stem rabbet as you determine it.

Bevels

Bevelling frames and transom consists in shaping their edges so that the planking will fit tightly against the frame its full width. The body plan from which the frames are built gives you the shape of the frame, and by a little

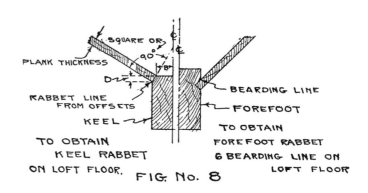

TO OBTAIN
KEEL RABBET
ON LOFT FLOOR.

TO OBTAIN
FOREFOOT RABBET
& BEARDING LINE ON
LOFT FLOOR

FIG. No. 8

applied geometry also the bevels. This is illustrated in Fig. No. 2. The square is stood up, "square off" the floor with the corner on the frame. The straight edge is held with lower end on next frame and intersecting the square at the same height above floor as the frames are inches apart on the profile or half-breadth plan. Obtain the bevel shown with a small bevel and mark it on a board or apply directly to the frame. This method assumes that the planking is straight from frame to frame and not curved, as is really the case, and for this reason is not absolutely correct but close enough.

Bevels may be roughly obtained directly from the plans or drawings; from the inboard profile, the bottom frame bevels, and from the half-breadth plan the side bevels. In case there is a bilge plank, as in *Fisherman*, the bevel here will be about halfway between the other two. After the boat is set up, as in Fig. No. 9, the entire frame will have to be faired off with plane and any errors in bevelling can be taken care of if not too great, therefore great accuracy here is not required. On large craft bevels are more vital and the loftsman makes what is called a bevel stick resembling a rule, and applies it across three frames to obtain the correct bevel of the middle one.

The house carpenter's bevel or try-square will do for a bevel, but a better and handier one for boat work is made by cutting in two a 12" boxwood ship carpenter's bevel. This makes two bevels, one about 4½" and the other about 7½" long. The smaller one is not much larger than a pocket-knife and the handiest tool imaginable.

Each frame piece must be bevelled inside and out in the vise before assembling, and do not make the common mistake of bevelling all the frames for one side of the boat, but get them out in pairs. Always remember that the bevel is applied to or placed on the moulding or laid-out face of frame which in turn is the side or face represented by the frame or station line on the plan. A glance at the plan will determine whether the bevel is acute and "under," or obtuse and "standing," as the boatbuilder would say. Also if one piece is under bevel its mate on the other side will also be under bevel.

The Chine and the Batten Keel

The chine or knuckle piece in a vee-bottom boat is usually shaped as in Fig. No. 4, with bottom and side plank rabbeted into it. Quite often it is made in one piece, but is easier worked and much easier bent by using two members, an inner and outer chine. This is standard practice in many boat shops and is incorporated in the plans shown here. In several of the smaller boats the outer chine is omitted and the plank lap at chine corner.

The notch for the inner chine should be cut in frames before they are erected. Fig. No. 4 shows a method of laying this out. The corner angle is first bisected as shown by measuring the spots Y and Z equidistant from the chine corner, and from these intersect equal arcs and draw the line D–E. Next mark off the plank thickness if not already done; parallel to D–E and on each side of it mark the outer chine half-breadths represented by A. The lines marked O, which represent the edge of plank, can now be squared in from the intersection and the inner face of outer chine

drawn in. From this line the inner chine thickness (B on the sketch) and its width (C) are laid out. It is necessary in order to provide sufficient plank landing to taper in width (A A) the outer chine. The taper will start at second or third frame for'd and is specified in the plans. This taper should be laid out on a board and used in laying out frame notches of these first frames.

Where outer chine is omitted and inside chine only is used, the procedure is much the same. The plank thickness is deducted first and the inner edge laid out square from the line D–E. The width C remains constant, but the thickness F will narrow from the second or third frame to about seam batten size at stem.

In any case the frame corner piece or gusset (see Fig. No. 5) is not cut out for but is placed against the chine as shown, and receives the chine fastenings, which are always screws.

What has been said above closely applies to runabout keels and keel battens, and they are laid out in a similar manner. The line D–E is already laid out and is represented by the body-plan centreline. The inner chine and keel batten both butt against transom and let into transom frame, the outer members only extending through in the same manner as planking.

The outer chine and keel are screw fastened to the inner member with marine glue between. The screws should be spaced closely enough to pull the two members tightly together everywhere, probably about six or eight inches apart, depending on the thickness of the two members. Counterbore for screw heads deep enough to allow for rounding off corner later.

If chine notches are laid out properly the inside chine may be fastened in place and except for taper for'd be fashioned on the boat. The outer chine should be worked on the bench from the dimensions previously obtained, and may be faired up with a rabbet plane when in place. The notches should be cut a little small and trimmed up after boat is erected, bevels corrected, etc., using batten.

Patterns

For many boats no frame patterns are required, but frame lumber can be laid out with less waste with their use, especially if it is knotty. For smaller craft heavy paper or cardboard are generally used, and in larger boats template lumber. In some cases all frame floors are the same shape, varying only in length; in which case mark out the longest one first and use it as a pattern; this applies also to deck beams. Where floors vary in shape they may be laid out with a straight edge by marking their width each side of centreline on the straight edge, and also the height of knuckle or chine above the frame at centre on it. In other words, the rise of floor. Cut the floors and all other frame members a bit long to allow for trimming when they are assembled, and mark chine, sheer, centreline, etc., on all patterns.

Lines may be transferred directly to lumber and to template lumber by the use of carpet tacks or nails. Lay them with heads on the line and body or stem of tack at right angles to it. Place about one and one-half or two inches apart and press the board you desire marked firmly on the tacks, remove the boards and the tacks or tack marks will be imprinted thereon, and by drawing a line through these marks you will have the shape transferred from floor to lumber.

When marking frames from patterns just remember that after marking one piece you must turn pattern over for marking its mate, if in pairs, as are the side pieces. If no patterns are used, mark one piece from its mate, keeping them face side to face side and the bevels will then come out right. Referring to Fig. 5 and assuming we are getting out frame No. 3 shown, mark the first side piece by pressing it on the tack heads, cut out and bevel this piece; now get out lower piece of frame in same manner. Place these last two on the lines face down and fit together at chine and cut bottom piece off on centreline, also cut chine notch; now use these pieces as patterns for other side of frame. When assembling frame the first-mentioned pieces will be placed face up on the left side, and last two pieces face up on right-hand side. On wood patterns, such as used for larger keels and stems, marks may be transferred from one side to the other of the pattern by drilling through with small drill. In this manner the rabbet and bearding lines are transferred and also transferred to the lumber by prick punching through each of these holes with a nail. Pattern lumber is best of some soft wood, such as pine or cedar, and easiest worked if from 3/16″ to 3/8″ thick, though thicker will do.

Cutting Out the Frames

A band-saw is of course best for this purpose, but one can do much with a sharp rip-saw, using a keyhole saw for the curves. With a bevelling band-saw or canting table the bevels may be sawed right on the frame, and the same may be done quite closely with a rip-saw by trying the bevel now and then; leave a little to trim on and cut all ends long.

Assembling the Frame

This is done as before mentioned on the body plan. Make sure that each piece of the frame has sheer, chine, centreline, or other reference marks on it. The set-up line must be plainly marked on the floor as shown in Fig. No. 6. As only one-half of the frame is laid out on the floor, the other side will have to be marked. It is not necessary to actually draw this half in, but locate the chine or knuckles and sheer and drive nails at these points (see Figs. Nos. 5 and 6).

The side members are generally tacked in place first; as the moulding or laid-out side of frame proper is almost invariably up, its edge must be squared down to the frame line on floor as in Fig. No. 3. In case frame floor is shown lapped over side pieces as in *Fisherman* it must be placed on top of side pieces, in which case moulding side will be down and can be squared up from floor line with square end block (see Figs. Nos. 3 and 6).

Often the whole frame lays flat on the floor and gusset pieces lap the corners and separate floor pieces connect the frame at centreline. This type of frame is shown in Fig. No. 5. In this case and taking frame No. 3 as an example, the right-hand side of frame is first fastened together on body

plan and face up, omitting the floor piece. This half is turned over and the other half of frame assembled on it back to back. The two halves are then placed in position on the floor as shown and floor piece and cross-band fastened in place.

By all means use waterproof glue in frame laps and fasten together with screws. The glue will add greatly to strength of joint and the screws will make possible a tight joint, so necessary for effective gluing.

It might seem logical to place the moulded face of frame against the floor with its edge on the line; this would eliminate any squaring up as in Fig. No. 3. Frames are often assembled in this manner, but a rougher job generally results, as any errors in frame bevels are just doubled by gussets and floor pieces. The frame or station line in the body plan intersects or divides two layers and represents the shape of both, and greater accuracy results if both layers are assembled to it.

The cross-bands may be 1″ × 4″, 2″ × 4″, or any common dimension stock, and if boat is erected upside down they should in many cases be the same width, as one edge is often on the set-up line and the opposite edge rests on the stringer (see Fig. No. 5). In Figs. Nos. 6 and 10 the width is immaterial.

Stem and Forefoot

In skiffs and similar construction the stem and forefoot are in one and are simple affairs, with no rabbet to cut. Each side is bevelled from centre of face, as dimensioned on stem detail or determined from the mould loft, or else this can be left until stem is fastened in place. In the latter case use a batten extending aft several frames to obtain the correct side bevel. Do not bevel stem sides above the sheer mark unless stem cuts off there, but keep a little away from it and trim to mark later when the sheer or top plank is put on. This will leave a square stem head to fasten face piece to; also make stem a bit long and round off or ogee later when boat is planked.

The larger boats have a rabbeted stem, the stem rabbet and bearding line are laid out in stem detail plan or determined in the mould loft, as explained under "Lofting." It is best to make forefoot and stem pattern of light template wood and fit them together just as they will go on the boat; also fit to keel pattern if the boat has a keel proper. Mark on the pattern the rabbet and bearding line; probably best done with tack heads as explained under "Patterns." After stem and forefoot are bolted or fastened together, mark and cut the rabbet.

As shown in Fig. No. 7 a square-end piece of wood, the same thickness as planking, is used as a template and the rabbet chiselled out until deep enough so that top of template is flush with rabbet line and lower surface is on bearding line. Cut a spot like this every six or eight inches and then trim out between the spots.

In case the builder is not sure of himself the above may all be done after the boat is set up, using a batten the same thickness as planking for a gauge, much the same as in Fig. No. 7. The batten is allowed to extend aft about two frames and represents the planking. Nothing is saved by this method, however, as it is much easier done on the bench. Waterproof glue should be used in all joints, and a handy method is to glue up the members and when glue is set properly put in the fastenings. In case the stem face is too narrow for the bolt heads they may be ground off on each side and a narrow slot chiselled in stem face instead of counterboring with a bit. The diameter of carriage-bolt heads is given elsewhere.

Stop-waters are generally placed where rabbet crosses stem, keel, and forefoot joints. These should be about ⅜″ or ½″ diameter, dry-pine dowels. A hole is bored through the joint and a tight-fitting stop-water driven through and cut off flush on each side. Fig. No. 11 shows two stop-waters; their purpose is to prevent the water creeping up the joint and forming a slow leak. If a proper glue joint is made they are not necessary, and many boats are built without them, but as a precautionary measure, they had best be put in.

Limbers

Some means must be provided for drawing the water that collects in the bottom of the boat to a central point, where it may be bailed out. This is done by cutting notches in the underside of the frames, called limbers. Their location and approximate size for different types of boats are shown in plans of *Vagabond, Camper, Sunray,* and Two Skiffs. They are most easily cut while assembling frames.

The Keel

Many small boats do not have what could be strictly termed a keel; instead this member is represented by a skeg or an exterior chafing strip, and in the runabouts by little more than a batten. The sloop *Vagabond* and cruiser *Mariner* shown in this book illustrate the true keel, and in such cases a pattern must be made from the mould loft door. In the case of the sail boat this will include the entire keel, forefoot, and stem, but in such boats as the cruiser the straight part may be represented by a batten, and a pattern made for the forward end only. Lower edge of batten will represent the bottom edge of keel, and offsets may be marked on it to top of keel and rabbet line. Be sure to mark all frame or station lines on keel pattern or batten to be transferred to keel itself.

Fig. No. 8 shows method of obtaining keel rabbet, or rather the inner rabbet and top of keel. In deducting the plank thickness on body plan the rabbet line is squared up from plank as shown, and its intersection with inside of planking will be the top of keel. The height *D* is then transferred to profile plan at each station and a batten bent to represent top of keel. The keel pattern is made to it and the distances *D* marked on pattern and at each station the width *B* is noted on pattern and later transferred to top of keel. This distance is also the half-breadth of the frame heel.

The keel rabbet should be cut before setting up and finished smooth with a plane. Keels of this type need not be of clear lumber, and the grade called "select common" is generally ordered. Any knots must be hard and sound, and in laying out the keel try and avoid their coming in the rabbet.

The runabout keel and keel batten are dealt with under "Chine and the Batten Keel," they being so similar in construction.

The Transom

The simpler transom is cut from one wide board if obtainable, or of two narrower boards glued together. In gluing, be sure the joint is tight, wood to wood, and clamp up, using door clamps if available. If not, lay the transom flat on the floor or bench and resort to wedges against cleats nailed fast to floor or bench top. If door clamps are used, a straight piece or two should be clamped flat on one side of transom to prevent buckling; use waterproof glue.

The larger transoms are built up on a frame. A pattern of one side (port or starboard) of transom is made and after the planks are jointed and set tightly together they are marked from the pattern and cut to shape. The laid-out or moulded side is, of course, the aft side, and the fastenings are through the plank into the transom frame. Counterbore for plugs and screw fasten. The two side pieces of frame are generally fastened first; the other members are then tacked in place, the transom turned back again, and the fastening completed. If the lumber is dry and the transom is to be varnished, the joint may be glued, as it is in the finest runabouts. If painted, it is just as well to provide a caulking seam and caulk it. The frame may well be glued to planking in addition to the regular fastening. A transom is laid out in detail in the plans for *Sunray,* an outboard runabout. Make the beam camber mould before laying out the transom or cut out a beam and use it to lay out top of transom.

Chapter IV

Erecting

Setting Up or Erecting the Boat

THIS IS THE boat-shop term for assembling or erecting the frame of boat, including stem and keel. Figs. Nos. 9 and 10 illustrate two methods of doing this. Wherever practical small boats are erected bottom up. This avoids practically all awkward upside-down work. Some jobs do not lend themselves well to this method and must be built in the erect position.

Erecting the Boat Bottom Up

We will assume that the centreline is marked on cross-band and floor of frames, and that stem, transom, and all other members are ready to assemble. Referring to Fig. No. 9, the two erecting stringers may be any common dimension stock, such as 2″ × 4″, 2″ × 6″, or 2″ × 8″, either new or used, and they need be straight on upper edge only. These are set up on some convenient erection and at the height most suitable for working on the boat. While shown on horses, blocks of wood or anything solid will do. The stringers are fastened in place at the distance apart specified in the plan, and the horses or blocking adjusted so that they are level and "out of wind" when sighted across their tops from one side. All must be securely fastened, including horses to floor.

Lay off the frame stations from plan on one stringer and square them over to the other. Cut the stringers off at transom, allowing for its thickness and also the slant or rake, if shown; two cleats must be fastened here to support the transom, as in Fig. No. 9, and must, of course, take the same rake before mentioned.

Put up transom, first centring it between the stringers and with set-up marks at proper height at or above stringers. Next, stretch a chalk line from transom centre to centre mark (between stringers) for'd, as shown in the illustration. This is for centring the frames and saves much measuring later, and also takes care of any side bend in the stringers. The frames are set up with centreline on the string, and be sure they are placed on the correct side of the station line, and then toenail cross-bands to stringers. They must be braced to transom by a ribband on each side of frame, as shown; these must be kept clear of the first plank, which is generally placed on the bilge.

The fore-and-aft position or rake of stem is located from the centre of the first frame, as shown by the arrow in Fig. No. 9. The stem must also be plumbed athwartship or sideways, either with a level or by extending a straight edge through several cross-band centres. Fasten permanently to frame or frames, as the case may be; in the illustration it is also secured by a cross piece to the stringers and braced to the floor. As planking exerts quite a side strain a rigid job is quite essential or the stem will wind up with a permanent side set. This applies also to the first frame, which should be well secured to the stringers.

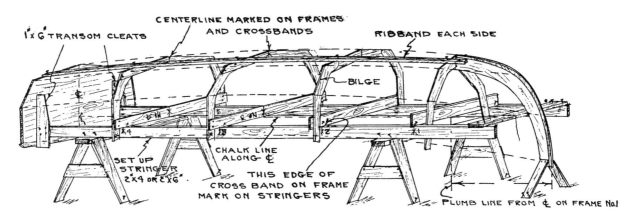

FIG. NO. 9 BOAT ERECTED BOTTOM UP — READY TO PLANK.

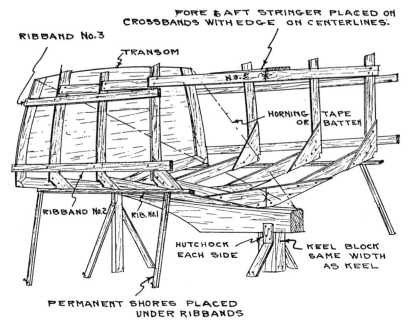

Erecting Right Side Up

Referring to Fig. No. 10, the keel is first set up and at the same rake or slant from base line, as shown in plans; this will set boat on an even keel. The keel blocks are cut to allow for this, and should be of sufficient height above floor to permit planking the bottom. If top of keel at lowest point is kept about two feet six inches above floor, both bottom and top sides will be at a convenient height, although for skidding around under the bottom convenient is a poor word. Blocks should be same width as keel and of sufficient number to support it without sagging between them.

A chalk line is snapped on the floor and keel blocks set to it, erecting only those under straight part of keel bottom. They must be plumbed with a level and braced about as shown. Fasten to each side of blocks a cleat or hutchock, shown in Fig. No. 10. Assuming that stem and keel are bolted together as per plans, the whole may be set on the blocks and fastened there through the hutchocks. Plumb and brace the stem and if possible run braces to building wall or ceiling joists, thus doing away with bothersome side and front shores, always in the way. Plumb the keel side with a level and use chalk line again alongside to detect any kinks which should be shored out. If there is a horn-timber or over-hang of keel aft or of stem for'd, this may be plumbed to our original chalk mark on floor and braced as shown in Fig. No. 10.

The aft end of keel may now be cut to take the transom, and do not make the common mistake of whacking the keel right off, but leave the shoulder underneath as shown in construction plans and which represents the planking. Set the transom at the proper rake, plumb it with a level on the centreline and place a temporary shore each side, to be replaced later by the permanent ones shown in the illustration. It must now be horned; this consists in stretching a tape or batten from centre of keel to the two upper corners or sheer marks on transom, as shown by the dotted lines.

Swing transom until each corner is equidistant, which accurately squares it with the ship. Brace in this position, keeping braces aft or clear for erecting balance of frames.

Starting with the next frame for'd, the balance of frames may be set in place and a temporary shore placed on each side. They must be plumbed by using a level on the cross-band and be spaced correctly at sides. As they are set up correct any error in bevel where frame fits keel and toenail to keel, allowing for keel bolts later.

A wide board with one straight edge (one of the bottom planks will do) is quite often tacked on top of cross-bands with straight edge on centreline. This runs from stem to transom and automatically ties the whole together (see Fig. No. 10). In many cases it is found expedient to set up every other frame and drop in the others after the ribbands are in place.

The ribbands shown under bottom, well out to the corners, should be put on first, and permanent shores are fitted under them about as shown. Ribbands vary in size with size of boat. For the larger boats shown here about 1¼″ × 1¾″ will do, and for the smaller ones ¾″ × 1½″, or whatever similar size is obtainable. They must be fairly clear, as the for'd end is subjected to quite a twist. This end may be tapered to aid in bending, and fasten the ribband to each frame with a common nail, driving it right home; it will pry off quite easily later. Start ribbands at stem rabbet, and as their function is to draw the frames fair, do very little dubbing or fairing off of frames, but pull frames to the ribbands.

The outside lower ribbands are now fastened in place and the frames may be tapped to one side or the other to aid in fairing up. Holes for keel bolts may now be bored through frame floors and keel; bore same size as bolts (no drift). These are shoved up from below and countersunk under keel. Galvanized carriage-bolts are best, and put a cotton grommet around each bolt before driving it home to forestall any possible leaks under bolt head; set up on washers on top of frame floors. Where keel is deep, drift bolts are used, in which case the hole in keel is bored 1/16" small.

The top ribband should be kept well up to the top, as shown, to clear the first plank, which is generally just below the sheer strake, and by loosening a few cross-bands where needed much unevenness may be removed. This finishes the procedure of setting up, and if properly done each ribband should be free from bumps, forming a fair line and the whole structure rigid and well braced.

Planking the Boat

The various woods suitable and commonly used for boat planking and the grade or quality specified are explained under "Boatbuilding Woods." In ordering this item it quite often happens that floor boards, seats, etc., are planking thickness, in which case the whole are combined in the order and the best selected for planking. Where subjected to hard bends, steaming is resorted to, but it is not required in most of the plans shown here. A practical and easily built steam box and boiler are described herein, and it does not pay to try to hang plank cold when they should be steamed. Hot water and sacks, however, are sometimes substituted for steam, as described under "Steaming Plank and a Steam Box."

Side plank, except in skiffs and similar construction, should not be of greater width than 5½"; 5" is better. Hot weather will shrink the driest lumber, loosening putty and caulking, and by keeping plank narrow this trouble is minimized. Bottom planking may be wider, up to 7½".

The general procedure is to start the bottom with the garboard, which is the plank next to keel, and to start topsides with the sheer strake or next plank down to clear top ribband, unless boat is built upside down. This necessitates two shutters or closers if the boat has an outer or rabbeted chine. Fig. No. 11 shows a simple method of laying out the garboard, and a similar method is employed for the shutters, as follows: The dividers are set to width of gap at inside edge of plank and these various widths scribed on a batten tacked just above or below the gap. Later the batten is tacked on the lumber and widths transferred to it. A good procedure is to bevel and fit one edge of plank first and then apply the widths from this finished edge.

In laying out a garboard the upper edge of batten represents the top edge of plank, also centre of seam batten. The dividers are swung in an arc to rabbet and the widths scribed on the batten. The batten is then placed directly on the board, top edge to top edge, and the widths rescribed on the plank. A narrow batten is sprung to intersect the widest points of these arcs. The widths should be taken with the compasses or dividers to the outer edge of rabbet; thus the face side of plank is laid out. In Fig. No. 11 the for'd end of batten is shown forming a pattern against the stem, and generally a pattern is made of the first few feet. In any case the pitch mark shown is transferred to plank to give exact fore-and-aft location of plank when putting it on the boat. The layout batten should be fairly wide and lay naturally in place on the boat, as any edge set will be transferred to the plank.

In laying out planking the widths should be kept uniform or graduate evenly. Long narrow slivers and finely tapered points should be avoided, as they are hard to caulk and fasten properly. A plank that increases in width as it nears the stem or stern is called a fish tail; also very poor form except in the garboards. The bugbear of planking is edge set or edge bend, and when this becomes at all pronounced the plank must be "spiled" or curved to fit. The shape is obtained with a fairly wide batten called a spiling batten; this batten is allowed to lay naturally (without edge bend) upon the frames in the same place as plank to be laid out, and offsets are then taken to the strake's edge against which the new plank will lay. When the batten is laid flat on the plank the offsets will give shape of new plank without edge set.

Planking Equipment.—The regulation boat clamp, such as shown in Fig. No. 12, is best for bending plank. One can get along with three or four, but more will save time lost in fastening off clamps and shifting. Four or six inch clamps are ideal, with one or two longer ones for long reaches; a door clamp or two about four feet long is very handy for edge set, especially in vee-bottom construction. In bent-frame boats a simple cast-steel jambing dog is used for edge-setting plank, but it cannot be used on deep sawed frames. Instead a small block is clamped on edge of frame as in Fig. No. 12 and the wedge driven against it. Make sure the clamp is firmly set up so that block does not move, otherwise it is sure to permanently twist the clamp.

Planking the Bottom.—The garboard is first, and as in all plank start it forward, clamping it to stem or forefoot

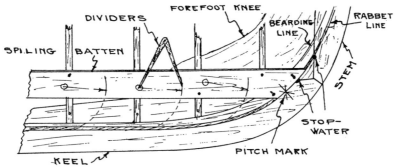

METHOD USED TO LAY OUT A GARBOARD OR A SHUTTER

FIG. No. 11

FIG. No. 12

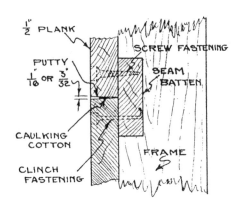

FIG. No. 13.

first. It may be kept an inch or so aft of the pitch mark to be tapped for'd later. This plank will probably offer your hardest twist, but with the thin plank encountered in small boats should give little trouble. Work it aft gradually, and if it does not fit properly leave it to cool and set, after which it will keep most of its shape and may be refitted at will without resteaming.

On widest frame between garboard and chine lay out the plank widths, being governed by lumber ordered for bottom planking. It would be a good plan next to tack a batten on the frames to represent the plank next the chine; its aft end may be quite narrow to avoid edge set. It is sometimes better if the batten is placed on the next plank inboard, in which case it will run further for'd and be a better guide to plank widths here. From it mark off plank widths on transom and note how widths will work out for'd, moving and adjusting batten to suit. These marks will be a guide in laying out the balance of planking, but need not be too strictly adhered to, as unexpected edge set, etc., may make a change advisable later.

While all the seam battens may be fitted in before planking is started, this would prevent changes in widths later. As you proceed with each plank a layout batten is tacked to frames representing its top edge, and from this the plank widths are measured and marked on the batten and later transferred to lumber. The top edge will also locate the centre of seam batten (see "Seam Battens"). It is not necessary that all bottom plank end on stem; in fact to do this would result in much cross-grain and waste of material. The for'd ends should be laid out to make planking as easy as possible, avoiding very wide ends and as much edge set as you can. After the chine is reached these ends may be screw-fastened to the chine.

All caulking seams should be tight on the inside edge, and for small boats a good ¹/₁₆″ or ³/₃₂″ wide on the outside, as shown in Fig. No. 13. Small tight seams should be avoided, as they are likely to be bruised in caulking. Varnished or natural finished topsides are not generally caulked from the outside, but the seam is run on inside of plank and a thin thread placed there. The planks should be closely fastened to the battens. In this case marine glue or thick paint should be applied between batten and plank and on plank edge (see "Caulking," also "Seam Battens"). The bottom is generally caulked in the orthodox manner.

Planking the Topsides.—The first thing is to lay out the plank widths amidship or at the widest point, which may be a little for'd of it. The sheer strake or one of the top planks close to it is generally hung first. If the boat is to be varnished the sheer strake must run to the stem, but may be tapered here to about 1¾″, thus greatly reducing edge set.

In case the boat is to be painted all plank need not end on stem. Locate with a wide batten the top edge of the first upper through plank to run from stem to stern and shift the batten, to avoid edge set. In this case divide and mark plank widths on transom and mark top edge of batten on each frame. We cannot as yet divide plank widths on stem, as the plank next the chine will probably end on stem with a narrow nib, so move the batten down to represent top edge of this plank, for which there is a spot marked on transom and midships. Plank widths may now be divided on stem and you can start planking at chine and work up, or start with the first through plank and come down. In the latter case put on seam battens for both edges of this plank before you start. Above this plank the for'd ends are allowed to end where they will naturally lay and are fastened to sheer batten or shelf.

Where the sheer strake runs to stem the first few upper plank will require spiling; use a wide batten as before mentioned. Divide the space at transom and midship to suit the number of plank and then move the batten down to represent top of chine strake, proceeding as described above for a painted job. In dividing the plank widths on stem the upper ones may be kept narrow, to eliminate edge set, and gradually increased as edge set disappears. An efficient method here is to fit and fasten seam batten first, being sure it forms a fair curve; then on the spiling batten you may mark not only the spiling, but plank widths obtained from centre of seam batten.

Wherever spiling curve requires too wide a plank, make the strake in two lengths, putting a butt-block at joint as shown in Fig. No. 14. A good rule to follow is that spiling curve should not exceed width of plank, *i. e.*, a 6″ plank from a 12″ board, this not only saves lumber but eliminates cross-grain. Lumps or unfair spots that appear in strake's edge should be taken off with a rabbet plane, and on larger boats the liner always inspects the strake's edge before laying out the next strake. All planks are made in pairs, and if a band-saw is used two are tacked together and sawed out at same time, one for port and one for star-board, shutters excepted. A piece of wood should always

14

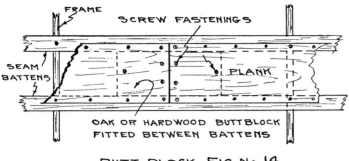

be placed between clamp toe and plank to avoid marking or splitting the plank.

Plank Fastening

Galvanized boat nails are as good as anything for fastening plank to deep oak frames; when tearing out for repair jobs the nail invariably pulls through the plank and remains unbudged in the frame. If you will examine one closely you will note that it has a chisel point; it must be driven so that this point cuts the grain of the frame, as it holds much better and is not so apt to split the frame. A rough rule for length of plank fastenings in hardwood frames is about 2¼ times plank thickness; by this rule ¾″ plank would require 1¾″ boat nails. In case the hull is to be finished bright (that is, varnished), the nail heads must be counterbored for and plugged; screws, however, are generally used in this case. Plugs may be obtained for any of the boatbuilding woods or made by yourself with a simple tool. Plugs must fit tightly, and as bits vary astonishingly in size it is best to try a few plugs first and not have a lot of holes for which special plugs must be made. For varnished finish, dip plugs in shellac as they are driven, and in white lead for painted hull. When hull is to be painted it is seldom plugged, but a leather punch slightly larger than the nail head is often used to break the skin, which allows the nail to sink neatly into the wood without splintering. Bore for each nail, and nail should fit tightly into hole; set deep enough for putty to hold, about one-eighth inch below surface. Copper boat nails, either to clinch or rivet, bend easily and should be drilled through both plank and frame or batten with a drill small enough that they will drive tight.

Screws are best in soft-wood frames and are also generally used in plank ends either at stem, transom, or butts. If nails are used in soft frames they must be larger, to compensate for the poorer holding power. A good rule for number of fastenings in each plank is to have one fastening for each two inches or fraction thereof; a 3½″ plank would require two, and a 5½″ plank three nails or screws to each frame crossing. Avoid bruising face of plank with hammer marks.

Seam Battens

Seam battens should be screw-fastened to the frames, but must not project through transom, but land on and fasten to transom frame. For'd the batten is notched or let into the stem sufficiently to form a good landing, and where seam batten ends on the chine it should be fitted against it and edge fastened. The position of the battens is governed by the planking.

Oak is ideal for this job, but as plank is either screw-fastened or through-fastened to the seam batten, soft wood is almost as good and is generally used. If the topsides are to be varnished or finished bright, no caulking seam is provided or else the seam is inside. In this case the battens should be glued to the planking and plank fastened before glue sets; glue should also be placed on plank edges. Some marine glues stain the plank badly but not deeply, so try and keep it off the plank face. Where planking is to be painted and caulked in the orthodox manner it is still desirable to glue the plank to the battens, but the seam must not be choked with glue, or more harm than good will result.

Planks are fastened to seam battens and chine with either screws or copper boat nails. These fastenings should be spaced from two inches to four inches apart, depending on plank thickness; closer for thin and wider apart for heavier planking. The varnished runabout is generally screw-fastened and plugged on the topsides.

Copper boat nails should be long enough to clinch over on the inside of seam batten, and except for very thin plank should be let in deep enough to take putty. They should be clinched as shown in Fig. No. 18 and as described under "The Dory Lap"; also see Fig. No. 13.

Deck Beams, the Shelf and Clamp

Beams are sawed from wide material to a specified crown or camber. This crown is a true arc or segment of a circle, and in small boats it can generally be swept in with a string or long rod and pencil by the well-known trial-and-error method. This is done much as you would scribe a circle with compasses.

Fig. No. 15 shows another method, which is as follows. Scribe a quarter circle, the radius being equal to the specified camber. Divide this quadrant and base into any number of equal parts (four are convenient) and join these points with straight lines as shown. Also divide the half-breadth of the beam into the same number of divisions and transfer the distances 1, 2, and 3 to their respective stations and spring a light batten between the spots. One of the longest beams is sawed to this shape and used as a beam pattern for the rest of beams or a beam mould is made of template wood.

It is good practice and a time-saver to give the deck beams a coat of paint before fitting them into the boat. Beams are bolted to the shelf (if provided) with galvanized carriage bolts and either screw-fastened or bolted to the frame heads. If they rest on a clamp they can only be toenailed to it from each side. Always fair up the original sheer marks by tacking a batten to them the full length of boat and sight it from various positions, adjusting it until it is fair to the eye, then strike in a new sheer line, which should not be much at variance with the original. The beam pattern is used to obtain top of shelf and clamp, after new sheer is run, by holding top of beam to sheer marks on

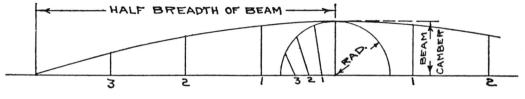

BEAM CAMBER OR CROWN FIG. No. 15

each side of frame and marking on it the top and bottom of beam. The bottom mark will be the top of clamp and sometimes top of shelf. It will in any case locate these two members. Keep top edge of clamp one-eighth inch or so above this mark to allow for fitting. It sometimes happens that the specified beam camber will not do for the first few beams for'd as it may form a bump in the deck, so leave these to the last and try the crown here with a batten on top of the beams and breasthook.

If frame heads are sawed off even with the line for top of beams, the material for shelf can be laid on these frame ends and marked to shape. When fitting it, try a beam here and there to see that it is set at the correct angle to suit beam camber.

If it is found necessary to remove the cross-bands to put in shelf clamp, etc., a new one should in each case be fastened in place lower down before the original cross-band is removed, so that boat will hold its shape.

Bulkheads

Waterproof plywood has largely replaced tongue-and-groove for small-boat bulkheads. It is equally as strong as the double diagonal tongue-and-groove bulkhead, is not as bulky, and can be installed with a fraction of the labor. A great deal of fitting may be saved by putting them in as early in the game as practical before they have to be fitted around seam battens, shelf, etc. As they are always placed on a frame, use the assembled frame as a pattern for shape of bulkhead before erecting the frame. Use glue between bulkhead and frame and fasten to frame with galvanized nails or screws. Edges of plywood should be well painted to minimize absorption of water in the end grain.

The Deck

There are several types of small-boat decks or deck finishes; the canvas-covered over tongue and groove decking, the caulked and varnished, and the battened and varnished decks.

The canvas-covered is the most practical and serviceable. The deck itself is of light tongue and groove, not wider than three inches. Start laying it from the centre with tongue outboard. A spline can be slipped between the two grooves on centreline; toenail at each beam and put a face fastening on the inner edge of each board. The latter are countersunk and puttied. The whole must be planed off and sanded before canvas is laid, and this is laid in thick paint or waterproof glue, the latter being the best. Use either the powdered casein or the ready-mixed glue and

apply with a paint brush to the deck. Lay the canvas, and starting from the centre, work or iron out the canvas toward each edge with a short flat board. Use much as you would an iron, but push out toward the edge, stretching it tight and working out to the edge all surplus glue. When all ironed out have some one pull it tightly down over the edge, gripping it with pliers and tack it all along the side (into shear strake), using galvanized or copper tacks. Leave the edge long enough so that after the guard is fastened the canvas may be trimmed off with a sharp knife run along its bottom edge. Place the tacks so that they are above this edge. The patent ready-mixed glue is often ironed with a hot iron, following the manufacturer's directions.

With the varnished deck a covering board is generally run around edge to stem. This may be tapered forward to about two-thirds its width. If there is no flush shelf provided to fasten deck ends to, then fillers must be fitted between the beams, as in the runabout *Tern*. The plank should not be much wider than 2¾" or thinner than ⅞6"; fasten to beams and fillers with screws or galvanized nails and counterbore for plugs. Caulk with a wheel (see "Caulking") and fill the seams with patent seam composition, or with putty colored to suit. Quite often the covering board is omitted and the deck ends are covered by the guard.

A combination of canvased and varnished deck is had with a varnished covering board, with canvas on balance of deck. The edge of the canvas is covered with a narrow hardwood strip about ½" × ¾" or so, screw-fastened on top and at inner edge of the covering board.

The battened deck is much the same as seam batten hull construction, and is shown in the outboard racer *Hornet*. The deck edges are glued to the battens and fastened with copper tacks clinched underneath. A covering board may be used or omitted as desired.

The latter construction is used chiefly on account of its light weight, the caulked deck for beauty. Any thin deck is hard to keep tightly caulked, and the varnished surface is easily marred. A canvased deck offers neither of these objections, though, of course, is not as handsome.

Caulking

Small boats are generally caulked with a caulking wheel. This simple tool consists of a metal disc about 1¼" or 1½" diameter, mounted on a handle in very much the same manner as the wheel on a caster. The wheel edges are quite thin and the cotton is laid on the seam and rolled tightly into it with the wheel. A caulking iron must be used at the stem and transom edges, and also for plank butts, etc. The

16

entire boat may be caulked with the iron, but it must be used carefully so that seams are not battered, or caulking driven right through the seam. Tuck the cotton in short tucks or gatherings, so that the threads will be somewhat across the seam, and do not just lay it fore and aft on the seam and then poke it in.

Caulking material is sold in two forms. One, the regular caulking cotton, consists of very loose "ropes" in no way woven or twisted. These may be divided into any desired size to suit the seam. The other, called candle wicking, very much resembles loosely woven string and comes in balls. Either may be used, but the former is preferable for most work and is purchased in one-pound hanks.

The seams in most small boats should be a sixteenth or three-thirty-seconds wide and tight inside, as shown in Fig. No. 13. Before starting sweep out all chips and dirt from the seams; also the floor should be swept clean around the boat in case some of the cotton drops or touches it. Linseed oil is generally brushed into the seams with a seam brush—an old toothbrush will do. The threads should be of such size that they will roll tightly into the seam and leave ⅛″ or 3/16″ for putty. A little experimenting will soon show how large the threads should be, probably the size of a small match when rolled tightly between thumb and forefinger. The same size will do also for the caulking iron; tap the iron lightly with a claw-hammer used on its side, and try and distribute the cotton evenly, avoiding lumps or bunches. The tendency at first is to use too large a thread, which either chokes the seam or if forced in damages it.

In skiffs and similar construction, caulking cotton or wicking is laid on edge of transom and side plank and up the stem. The side and bottom plank are then fastened against it. Small copper tacks are very useful in holding the cotton in place while fastening, and the cotton should be laid in thick paint. In drilling through plank for nails, try and keep clear of the cotton, as it wraps around the drill, leaving a hard lump around nail holes with no cotton between them.

By all means paint the seam after caulking, using a seam brush or toothbrush, and see that the cotton is well covered. This keeps moisture out of the cotton and provides something for the seam putty to cling to.

The modern way with battened seams and varnished topsides is to omit the caulking seam or put it on inside of plank; in the latter case a thin thread is placed along this edge and the next plank pressed against it. Sometimes a small groove is run along the edge of a soft string or twine placed in the groove (see "Seam Battens"). Very thin planking ¼″ and 5/16″ is seldom caulked, but depends on tight-fitting edges, the seam batten, and glue for water-tightness.

Breasthook and Knees

The old-school boatbuilder made these of natural crooks, but this is seldom done now, as they are hard to obtain and straight-grain hardwood serves very well. The crooked limbs in oak trees, vine maple, and other hardwoods made splendid crooks, and if any of these are available they can be used to advantage, for aside from their strength they make a nicer appearing knee with the grain following the curve as though they were grown for that particular job. They must be seasoned, but if roughed out will dry quickly. Avoid the heart, or the crook may be ruined by checking.

The breasthook in decked-over jobs need not be of hardwood and should be fastened through stem with a carriage bolt; also to each shelf if so constructed. As the stem face is generally too narrow to receive the full diameter of carriage-bolt head the head should be ground and a similar slot chiselled up and down in stem face to receive it. This is later puttied over and covered by stem band. Thwart or seat knees are screw-fastened from under the seat, also through planking, or else riveted to both. Transom knees are screw-fastened through transom and planking into the knee.

Dressing Off Hull

The hull should not be planed off until caulked and all seams and nail holes are puttied. Allow putty to harden a bit and then traverse with a sharp plane. Traversing is planing across the plank at an angle of about forty-five degrees or more. Plane just enough off the plank to take off caulking seam ridges and to touch the surface everywhere. Finish by planing fore and aft with a plane set fine and have a straight cutting edge on the plane bit, as a rounding edge will leave a lot of plane marks. Some plane off hull before puttying, but the open seam corners are then quite often damaged and a rougher job results.

The hull is next scraped with a cabinet scraper and then sanded. Sand first across the grain (unless for a varnished job) and then complete the job fore and aft. A wooden smoothing plane is much the best for boat work, and in fact all the boatbuilders' planes are of wood; but these are not commonly available and an iron plane will do quite well. A piece of thick cork such as is found in old life-preservers makes an excellent sandpaper block. The bottom, unless for racing purposes, merely has the rough spots and seam ridges planed smooth and then sandpapered.

Where the planks are flush-fastened, as in many light racing craft, the plank should be smoothed on the bench, as about all that may be done afterward will have to be done with a large flat file, sandpaper, and perhaps a little scraping.

Shaft Log and Engine Beds

The shaft line is best obtained on the mould loft floor by laying out motor and propeller in the profile lines plan. The engine manufacturer always furnishes an installation diagram, and the wheel diameter must be determined. Lay both out in the profile, allowing at least three-fourths inch clearance between tip of wheel and hull. Most marine installations are drained with a pump, so it is not necessary to allow clearance for draining crank-case. If an automobile motor is used, a sketch or template will have to be made showing shape and depth of crank-case, etc.

Where there is no outside shaft log, as in the typical runabout, the shaft line may be ascertained during construction. Before bottom planks are put on stretch a chalk line just clear of keel to represent the offset centre of shaft, and mark and cut the shaft hole before proceeding with the planking; also install the shaft log if of wood. The patent metal log may be installed later. Cut shaft hole through keel and keel batten with a gouge, and bore that through the shaft log on the bench. The hole should be at least three-sixteenths inch larger than shaft diameter. Bolt log through keel with carriage bolts and put a few extra screws in keel and keel batten at shaft hole.

When placing the engine beds, keep about one-half inch low to allow for a hardwood shim between engine beds and bed plate to aid in lining up motor.

Guards

These are always of hardwood and finished bright. Teak, bagac and mahogany are favorites. Oak is often used and will stand much abuse, but has one bad fault in that it does not "stay put" very well and checks badly. Where a guard is placed at edge of deck forward it is best to flatten off most of the flare, as shown in the shelf detail of the outboard cruiser *Mariner;* otherwise it is very hard to pull in the lower edge.

Fasten all guards with screws, and as it is almost impossible where decked over to use clamps the following method is used. The for'd end is fastened to the stem, and by putting a clamp on the aft end of guard a helper can give the piece any desired amount of twist, at the same time bending it in. It must be fastened and pulled up tight as you work aft, one screw at a time.

It is best to slightly hollow out the inside of guard so that both edges fit tightly against the canvas or against the plank face. Paint the inside of guard and put plenty of thick paint between it and the hull; if this is not done water will lodge underneath it and rot both plank and guard. The fastenings are, of course, plugged over, and should be long enough to penetrate the planking and grip the frame or shelf inside. If found necessary to make the guard in two pieces the butt should be at an angle, about forty-five degrees, sloping aft from inside; paint the joint well or the water will run in the end grain and ruin the finish around the butt.

The Stem Band

This is usually of galvanized-iron half-round or brass and fastened with flat-head screws. It must be bent before holes are drilled and countersunk, otherwise it will kink at the drill holes. It can be bent by poking one end in a convenient crack or in the vise. No pattern is needed; just bend and straighten until it fits fairly well—the screws will do the rest. Bend over stem head as shown in plans.

Cast stem bends of wedge-shape section are sometimes made, but chiefly for yacht tenders or expensive jobs, and require a wood pattern to exact shape, from which the stem band is cast.

Runabouts often have a brass sheet-metal cut-water of two pieces brazed together at the for'd end. Sixteen-gauge metal is about right. The aft edge is screw-fastened to

planking with screws closely placed, and the cut-water should be extended aft enough so that its fastenings will clear plank fastenings.

The first-mentioned or half-round stem band is the most practical for small boats, and except on runabouts is almost always used.

Lead Flashing

This may be purchased in rolls or cut from a sheet. It should be about 1¼″ to 1½″ wide and not less than ¹⁄₁₆″ thick. Form it into angle-iron shape by bending it over the edge of a 2 × 4; use thick paint or white lead under it and tack with galvanized or copper tacks—the latter are best. Place them about one-half inch or five-eighths inch apart and close to the edge to keep it tight against the wood or canvas. It may be bent around rounding corners by gently tapping the bottom flange and working or expanding the metal here.

Installing the Inboard Motor

Assuming that engine bed is in place and shaft line established, the next thing is to set the engine temporarily in place and as nearly in correct position as possible. The shaft should now be slipped in, blocked up in place, and the coupling faces bolted together. The stuffing-box should be slipped over the shaft before coupling is driven on. The strut or aft bearing can now be fitted and bolted on, and if a strut, then babbetted around shaft. The stuffing-box is fitted and bolted, after which break the coupling and reline the motor, using feelers and turning motor and shaft over to see that they line up in all positions. The feelers are thin strips of metal graduated in thousandths and are slipped between coupling faces to determine when these faces are parallel all around their circumference.

A space of about one-half inch to three-fourths inch is generally left between strut and propeller. Whether or not a muffler is installed, run cooling water into exhaust pipe close to motor to keep pipe cool; usually a very small amount is let in a few inches from the exhaust manifold, and the rest a foot or so farther down to avoid getting water in valves. The best outlet for exhaust pipe is out through transom just above the waterline. It must slope downward from motor, and motor end should drop abruptly for short distance to keep out the water; use forty-five-degree elbows.

Use copper tubing for gas lines (flanged fittings, not friction), and too much care cannot be exercised in seeing that all joints are tight, and they should be set up with shellac. A drip-pan covered with very fine copper screen should be placed under carburetor. The gas tanks should vent overboard and connect to filling plugs on the deck so that fumes do not drop down around tank when filling. The tanks themselves should be of galvanized metal heavy enough not to rust through in two or three years. Eighteen gauge is the lightest material advisable, and heavier is better; rivet and solder the seams. A valve should be placed

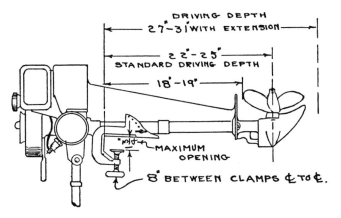

GENERAL DIMENSIONS OF THE AVERAGE OUTBOARD MOTOR

in line to motor, close to tank, so that gas may be shut off here.

Proper ventilation is vital in the engine compartment and some sort of vents should be installed to let air in and to draw it out.

Installing the Outboard Motor

The earlier motors were designed with varying lengths of drive shaft; the manufacturers have since, however, standardized their models to suit a transom sixteen inches deep. This shaft length was decided as most suitable for the average outboard boat. For large boats an extension piece can be purchased lengthening the shaft, in some models five inches and others six inches. The longer shaft should be ordered for large runabouts and cruisers.

In the plans shown here no depth of transom is specified, as it will, of course, depend upon the motor used. The cavitation plate must be submerged an inch or more and the tip of the propeller blades should be below the transom bottom. From bracket opening to centre of propeller on most standard models is from twenty-two inches to twenty-five inches, and deducting the half-diameter of propeller leaves about eighteen inches for the smaller and nineteen inches for the larger models. I would cut the transom (standard models only) to this depth and when in the water cut to suit trim of boat and cavitation plate. Cut about as shown in detail of *Sunray*, the outboard runabout. Some sort of stiffener or cleats must be provided on inside of the transom to take the motor clamps, and should have the grain running opposite to that of transom and be screw-fastened to it.

There are today many refinements to outboard motor-boating, and cruisers and runabouts can be fitted with remote control, and started, throttled, and steered from a forward-driving position. The fuel tank on the average motor contains fuel for about one hour at top speed; for long cruises auxiliary tanks may be installed and directly connected to the motor. This will be found much more convenient than refilling motor tank from time to time. In estimating the size of auxiliary tanks required, an allowance of one gallon per eight (8) horsepower per hour will be found about correct for the outboard. From this a sixteen (16) horsepower motor would require a twelve (12) gallon tank for a six (6) hour run. One gallon per ten (10) horsepower hours is generally allowed for the inboard motor, it being a little more efficient.

19

Chapter V

Finishing

Spar Making

THE BEST MATERIAL for small-boat spars, or for large ones for that matter, is spruce. Strength combined with light weight makes it ideal for this purpose. Fir and pine may be substituted, but are heavier, and put added weight where you are striving for lightness. Racing craft are equipped with hollow spruce spars in an effort to reduce weight of rig to the minimum.

The first operation in spar making is to strike a centreline on the stick, and from it lay out the spar dimensions as given on the sail plan. These dimensions divide the mast above deck into five equal parts and the height above deck is also given, but from deck to step should be measured from the boat. Tack a batten to the spots and square up the stick, fairing it up with a jack plane or jointer. It should now be marked off for reducing it to the "eighth square," as it is called, or to the octagonal. Fig. No. 16 shows a simple tool that may be made for this purpose. It is made from a piece of half-inch scrap, preferably hardwood, and the two points or markers are finishing nails driven in and filed to a point. It is dragged along the spar with vee-shaped ends kept tightly against sides of spar.

If a band-saw is available, the four corners may be sawed off by laying the stick in a vee-shaped guide, which holds it plumb, corner to corner, while being sawed. This guide is merely a block with a forty-five-degree notch

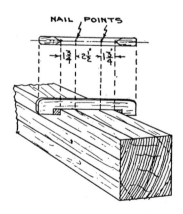

SPAR MARKER

FIG. No. 16.

sawed in its top edge into which the spar corner fits. A thin board is clamped across the saw table just in front of the saw to prevent the guide from sliding into the saw, but allowing it to slide freely sideways. A drawknife will do quite well if no saw is available.

The four new cuts or sides must now be planed up, and we have the spar in octagonal form. The rest is done with the eye, reducing the eight-sided shape to a round one, using drawknife and plane. For the final smoothing up a hollow or spar plane is best, but as it is seldom available a smoothing plane set fine will do, and finish it with sandpaper. If you have a piece of cork, hollow it to fit the spar and place the sandpaper in this hollow. The block may be hollowed out by placing a piece of coarse sandpaper on a pipe or can of the right diameter and rubbing the cork on it. This diameter will be the spar's largest diameter. Sand the spar with a twisting or corkscrew motion and not directly fore and aft.

Mast heels are generally fashioned into a large tenon which fits into a mortise in the mast step, and the mast is often left square at the heel, up to a few inches above deck, as it is easier to make and fit flat wedges than hollow ones. In small boats wedges may be dispensed with and a hardwood block with a fairly neat mast hole through it screwed to deck instead as shown for the *Flattee*. If the mast is to stay permanently in the boat a canvas skirt is often fitted over the wedges and lashed tightly around the mast and tacked around the edges to deck. If Marconi rigged, there will be a sheave mortised into mast near the top. A sheave from a cheap galvanized block will do, although brass and aluminum sheaves are manufactured for the purpose; the pin should be brass or bronze. This is kept from slipping out either by riveting a washer on each side or by two small brass diamond-shaped plates tacked or screwed on each side. (See *Vagabond* for a superior though less simple installation.)

Booms are generally connected to the mast by a gooseneck fitting, and if none is available the old-fashioned jaw, as detailed under *Truant,* may be substituted. Bore a drain hole in bottom of mast step if possible, as the mast tenon will rot quickly if water lodges in the mortise. Bore a hole through boom at aft end for the clew line to pass through; this is the line used to stretch foot of sail. Spars should be finished with three coats of good marine varnish.

Rigging

Unless the amateur is able to properly splice wire rope, this job is best left to a rigger. On small boats this item will cost but little, and the professional rigger will do it quickly and accurately. Unless the boat is intended for racing, galvanized-iron or cast-steel rigging wire is best. The racing sloops use aircraft strand, which is of much smaller diameter for the corresponding tensile strength, but the galvanizing is so thin that it soon rusts, and in addition it is hard to work. Iron rigging is the most durable and quite strong enough.

The loops around the masts should be served (wrapped tightly) with hard white twine and then shellacked, though they are often just taped; on fancy jobs they are covered with thin leather. The splices at the turnbuckles should also be served, but are sometimes taped and then shellacked or varnished. Where mast has a track on aft side this will hold the forestay from slipping, but elsewhere a cleat must be screwed on to serve the same purpose. Fig. No. 17 shows such a cleat. Lignum-vitæ is the best material, but any good hardwood will do, and fasten with brass screws. These cleats may also be purchased of cast bronze or galvanized iron.

Turnbuckles should be kept well greased, as the screw threads rust badly, and they should be the regulation galvanized or bronze rigging turnbuckles with lock nut on top and bottom to prevent untwisting. Purchase jaw and jaw turnbuckles and eliminate shackles; connect to shroud through a thimble spliced in the wire; there should be no turnbuckle on the forestay. Turnbuckles should be one size larger than the rigging wire.

The boom is best connected to mast with the regular gooseneck band, but the old-fashioned jaws will do, as detailed for *Truant*. These, if made of oak or ash, will match the spruce spar; be sure the grain runs as shown in sketch. Sometimes a set can be cut from around a large knot, placing the knot where the mast will be. In small boats a screw-eye can be placed in aft side of mast close to deck, and a lashing up to a screw-eye in the boom will keep it from climbing the mast. This, of course, is not needed with a gooseneck fitting.

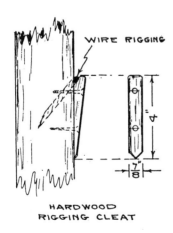

HARDWOOD
RIGGING CLEAT

FIG. No. 17.

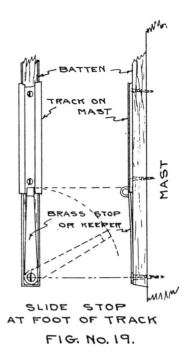

SLIDE STOP
AT FOOT OF TRACK
FIG. NO. 19.

The track on mast or boom for jib-headed or Marconi rig may be purchased at most ship chandlers or furnished by sailmaker, and is mounted on a narrow batten about three-eighths inch or one-half inch thick. The rigging-wire loops should be slipped over mast first and then notches cut out of the batten to accommodate them. It is sometimes necessary to shim out the batten above and below the wire if loop is very cumbersome. Fasten the track with brass screws and stop the track about eight inches above the boom in order to slip on the slides. A little brass keeper, see Fig. No. 19, must be placed on mast at bottom of track to prevent the slides slipping off when sail is down.

All rope should be manila, although a cotton main sheet is supposed to be "de luxe." Order blocks oversize, as rope diameters increase greatly with use. The jib sheet must lead so that it bisects the angle formed by the leach and foot, otherwise the sail will not draw properly.

Sails

This is a job for the sailmaker and you will find that you can spend much or little, depending on the material used. Sails are generally specified crosscut, that is, the cloths run at right angles to the leach on the mainsail and often the jibs are cut with cloths at right angles to both leach and foot, meeting on a line that bisects the angle formed by these two sides. In small boats, such as shown here, a rope is sewed along the mast and foot of mainsail, and the stay or luff of the jib; this should be ¼" diameter hemp bolt rope.

The sailmaker will sew on the jib snaps, also mainsail slides if used, and can supply tract to suit. Battens are generally made of hickory or oak, with pockets provided for them in the sail. I would suggest battens be about ¼" × 1½" tapered to about ⅛" thick at forward end.

A new suite of sails should be broken in gradually. Do not stretch them tightly all around but allow them to

THE FIRST SAIL

gradually take their proper shape. If this is not done the corners will elongate and the foot and leach take on a hollow or concave appearance. Note in the illustration the roach or curve in the aft edge or leach of mainsail (exaggerated a bit in the photo). Note also the unwrinkled corners and that there is plenty of stretch left for the sail at end of boom and top of mast.

Painting

In boat work cheap ingredients will not do. Use paint manufactured for the purpose or mix yourself of pure white lead and linseed oil. The raw oil is said to be superior for outside work, but dries very slowly, and for this reason the boiled product is generally used. Where the boat is to be kept in salt water for any length of time a copper or antifouling paint must be used from the waterline down. On no account put any other paint or priming coat on this surface, as it will simply mean that your copper paint will not stick, and the only remedy is to remove the offending oil paint. Two coats of copper are considered sufficient, and the last one should be put on just before launching. The interior of the boat should be thoroughly painted, not only for surface protection but to prevent absorption of water, which soon makes the boat heavy and loggy. Two coats are considered sufficient here.

After the first coat on the outside, all hammer marks, knots, and rough places in seam putty or hull should be smoothed over with a paste, using a broad putty knife. This paste is easiest made in small quantities, from commercial crack-and-crevice filler mixed with white lead ground in oil (not the dry) until it forms a smooth paste. The crack-and-crevice filler is handled by all paint dealers. It may also be made from the following recipe. Mix in dry form the following: 5 parts of zinc white, 3½ of whiting, 5 of litharge, and 9 of white lead, and bring to paste form by mixing with the following: 1 part varnish, 2 parts of dryer, and 1 of turpentine previously combined; by mixing a little

stiffer this is also a good seam putty. Either of the above pastes dries quickly and should then be sanded smooth and gone over again if need be. Still another recipe and a bit simpler is as follows: Mix dry white lead and whiting, half of each, then bring to paste form with Japan dryer and spar varnish, also about equal parts.

Do not try to put paint or varnish on in heavy coats, but rather use thinner ones and more of them. Have a clean, smooth surface and allow plenty of time for the paint to dry between coats (twenty-four hours at least). Take good care of your brushes, washing them out with gasoline, and avoid dust as much as possible.

Painting the Interior.—Use marine flat paint and add 5 per cent of turps for the first coat; apply two more coats, sanding between each. If a lustre finish is desired, thoroughly cover the work with flat paint and finish it with one or more coats of gloss or enamel.

Painting the Topsides.—Use exterior marine paint and thin the first coat with 25 per cent boiled linseed oil. Follow with two more coats full strength. Smooth up the surface after the first coat, using one of the pastes previously mentioned. A gloss finish is generally desired here, and is obtained by using gloss paint or, for a de luxe job, enamel. The latter is, by the way, not at all easy to put on, and like varnish requires warm weather or a warm room for good results. As a good gloss paint will give nearly the same lustre, I would pass up the enamel.

Painting the Racing Bottom.—Use hard-bottom racing compound and paint according to the manufacturer's directions on the can. A coat of good white-lead paint is sometimes used as an undercoating, but never an antifouling or copper paint. Sand with No. 00 sandpaper between coats and finish the final coat with powdered pumice stone and water rubbed with a felt or thick cloth pad. In the racing outboard or hydro, skin friction forms a large part of the total resistance, and a smooth bottom is of greatest importance. The same methods apply to the racing sailboat.

Painting the Canvas Deck.—Use deck paint and thin the first coat with 50 per cent boiled linseed oil; that is, two parts paint and one of oil. Follow with two coats full strength, sanding between each coat. Allow plenty of time to dry and brush the paint well into the canvas.

Puttying the Seams

After caulking, the seams and nail holes must be well painted, using a seam brush; if none is available an old toothbrush will do. Be sure the cotton is well covered as it keeps the moisture out of it and also provides a suitable surface for the putty to cling to. The putty is pressed in with a putty knife, care being taken to see that it reaches the full depth of seam. The boatshop uses a putty gun, which is a brass pipe fitted with a plunger and flattened to a narrow slit at one end. The pipe is filled with putty and the plunger firmly pressed in as the slit end is slid along the seam, filling it with putty.

The dictionary defines putty as a mixture of whiting and linseed oil, but in late years a cheap oil (sometimes fish oil) has been substituted. These inferior oils will often penetrate the paint and mark each seam with a dirty brown streak, and such putties should not be chanced for marine work. White-lead putty, as it is called, can generally be purchased at marine hardware stores; if not available, mix linseed-oil putty and white lead in equal quantities. Use the dry white lead and bring to proper consistency with addition of varnish; very little is required. Under "Painting" is given a formula for smoothing compound which, if mixed a little stiffer, is also an excellent seam-filler, and there are several very good patent compositions on the market. Putty may be colored by mixing in a little powder or paste color and can be thus made to match any natural wood finish.

Do not use putty in shallow dents and rough spots, but use the smoothing compound as described under "Painting." Putty, if too sticky, can be made more workable by the addition of a little whiting.

The Varnished or Bright Finish

Varnish when in contact with salt water seems at best short-lived, and the proper application of the first few coats has much to do with results later on. It is general practice to treat the wood with some filler before varnishing; this is wiped off and leaves a dull, smooth surface and fills the pores in the wood. While it makes a very nice-looking job, it has, from the standpoint of utility, an objectionable feature for outside work. The filler forms a film between varnish and wood and prevents the varnish from obtaining a proper hold on the wood itself. It is claimed that more lasting results are obtained by applying the varnish without filler. This theory is by no means new, and the chief objection to it is that it requires an additional coat or two at the start.

If avoidable, do not varnish on a cold day; the varnish will run in spite of all the brushing you may do, and will go on in a heavy, uneven coat. The hotter the weather the better, and out in a hot sun it will dry hard in half an hour and brush on like so much thin oil. Allow at least twenty-four hours between coats, and sand lightly or use steel wool, putting on three or four or more coats to build up a thick protective coating which will last.

Later, when revarnishing, wash the surface clean, using a refined soap, a sponge, and warm water. Rinse with clean water and when dry sand the surface lightly. It is sometimes impossible to pick your weather, and when cold it helps to set the varnish can in a larger vessel of hot water. Revarnish before the bare wood shows itself anywhere, and if possible keep the boat under cover. On large yachts the dew is chamoised off every morning before the sun gets at it, so important is it to give the varnish every possible aid. The same rules as to drying time, dust, clean brushes, etc., apply here as to painting, but to a much greater degree, and to dust particularly.

Varnishing the Interior.—If on soft wood, apply a coat of good grade liquid wood-filler and allow twenty-four hours to dry. Sand lightly and after wiping off the dust apply two coats of varnish. For hardwoods use the paste filler as per directions on the can and when wiping off work across the grain. A rubbed finish may be obtained by rubbing the final coat with raw linseed oil and powdered pumice stone or water and the stone. For a stained finish, first apply a good oil stain to the bare wood, using a liquid filler afterwards for soft wood and a paste filler for hardwoods. The latter may be colored to match by mixing in a little of the oil stain.

The Exterior and Topsides.—If the planks are not of uniform shade and do not match well, apply an oil stain, following directions. Wipe to a uniform shade, and when quite dry (twenty-four hours should be allowed) you may apply a filler if you wish. Use the liquid filler for soft woods, and the paste for hardwoods; just as for the interior finish above. Three coats of the best exterior or spar varnish should be applied, sanding lightly between each.

Varnished Decks.—The same procedure is followed here as for the topsides except that a filler is seldom used and that the first coat may be thinned with about 5 per cent turpentine.

Running the Waterline

The waterline is shown on the drawings and the paint line should be a few inches above the designed waterline or line

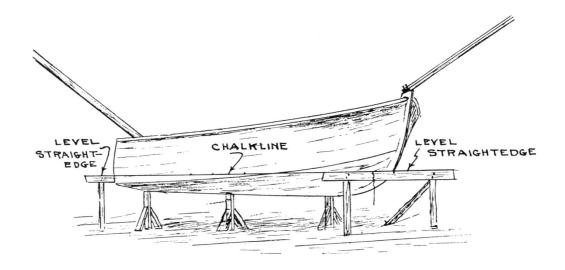

of flotation, and a bit higher for'd than aft. It is transferred to the hull by the following method. Determine its height at bow and aft; across transom tack a batten or straight edge with top edge on the waterline and level; it should project a foot or so each side. Do the same across face of stem and make this one a bit longer than width of boat. A chalk line is now stretched across tops of straight edges so that it touches the hull about amidships; the ends are gradually drawn in and a finish nail tacked every foot or so to mark the line and prevent it rolling down.

The chalk line may be dispensed with by having some one sight across the top of straight edges while you hold a pencil against hull and move it up or down as directed by the sighter. In either method a batten is then tacked to spots and the waterline marked in; this is best scratched in so that it is not obliterated by subsequent coats of paint; use a back saw for this purpose.

Chapter VI

Miscellaneous

Marine Glue

ANY GLUE SUITABLE for boatbuilding must, of course, be impervious to water. There are two kinds in common use, one ready-mixed and of similar appearance to the household variety, the other is sold in powdered form and is a casein glue and so called. The former is ready to use and directions for its use are furnished by the manufacturer. The latter is mixed with cold water, and proper mixing is very important. There are many different kinds, but the following instructions will pretty well cover the mixing of most of them in the small amounts used in building a small boat. An egg beater is the most satisfactory mixer, and will not be damaged for culinary use. Add the glue to the water slowly to avoid lumps; mix two or three minutes and the glue will become heavy and stiff; allow to stand for twenty minutes or longer, during which chemical action takes place. The glue now begins to thin down. Thoroughly mix again and allow to stand thirty minutes or longer before using. Some brands are good for two or three days, others must be mixed fresh every day.

Properly fitted and tightly clamped, a glue joint in soft wood will hold the fibres so tightly that a fracture will occur adjacent to rather than in the joint itself. Glue is used for making one wide board of two narrow ones, as for transoms, etc., for hollow spars, and to fasten canvas to the deck. Its judicious use throughout the ship at frame joints, etc., will add greatly to the strength of the boat.

A glued joint to be effective must be in dry lumber, be tight wood to wood, and clamped up with sufficient pressure, the more the better. Boat clamps and door clamps are best, and by proper planning they need be tied up only over night, which is sufficient time for glue to set provided the piece is not too roughly handled; twenty-four hours is better. Keep casein glue off painted surfaces, as it is a fair paint remover; also it will stain the surface of bare wood but not deeply. This should be kept in mind where a bright or varnished finish is intended.

The Dory Lap

This is so called because of its extensive use in fishing-dory construction. It is easily made and by its use very wide boards, so expensive and often impossible to obtain, are not necessary. The lap should be roughly twice the width of the plank thickness. In Fig. No. 18 one-half-inch plank is shown with a one-inch lap. This should be gauged on the planks and worked off on the bench, being careful to obtain a flat surface free from bumps. The edge of the planks must be fairly straight or trouble will occur when they are put together.

Paint the contacting surfaces of the lap, or, better still, use marine glue, and after the planks are in place on the boat the lap should be fastened before paint or glue sets. Use square copper boat nails long enough to clinch on the inside, about one-fourth inch over length will do. Bore for each, using a drill slightly smaller than the nail, and space about one and one-half inches apart for half-inch planking, and a greater distance for heavier material. Drill a large number of holes, stick a nail in each one and then drive the lot. When starting the nail through the hole the "hold on" should be held a little "squejee," as shown in the sketch; this starts the point on the clinch and then ends up with the iron solid against the wood. If this method is not followed the nail may just buckle in the middle and not clinch at all; also this gives some control over the direction of the clinching point. A stub end of shafting or maul head make excellent head ons.

When painting or varnishing the boat allow the paint or varnish to run into the lap, and turn the boat over if necessary so that it will do so. This makes for watertightness and is always done in lap-strake boats.

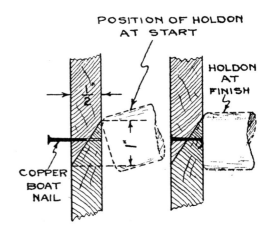

THE DORY LAP

FIG. NO. 18.

Steaming Plank and a Steam Box

A small steaming outfit is easily made, and if there are many hard bends to make it is certainly worth the bother. As just the for'd ends of plank need steaming, an eight-foot box will be long enough for most small boats. It may be made of two pieces of 1 × 4 and two 1 × 12, making a box 3½" × 10" inside dimensions, or it may be made of any suitable odds and ends; leave one end open. If a thread of cotton is laid in the joints it will aid greatly in making them tight. The best boiler I have found is an old range boiler so often found knocking around vacant lots. This will no doubt have a small leak, but unless too large will not bother, as there will be no pressure against it. There will be two holes in one end which must be plugged, and a short piece of pipe or a nipple screwed into the hole in the side. The boiler is then propped up on its flat with side hole up, and an improvised firebox built along each side. I have seen some just dig a trench which forms the firebox, and the boiler is laid lengthwise of it. It is sometimes desirable to have the steam box in the basement, in which case a more thorough job will be required; also a stovepipe connected to a flue.

In any case a hole is bored in the centre of the box and it is set on its flat over the nipple or pipe that was screwed in side of boiler. It may be set at right angles to boiler to avoid burning the ends. Screw a street ell in the one remaining hole, which will be in the centre of what was formerly the bottom end. The ell should point up and is used to fill with water, and do not put in too much, about one-third full is plenty. The ell is plugged with a cork or by putting a block of wood over it; do not screw in a pipe plug. If a de luxe job is desired, drill two small holes in end for try cocks and plug them with hardwood pegs. A range boiler may be substituted by a small oil drum or other similar drum or tank.

The old rule is one hour steaming for each inch of plank thickness, but this depends upon the efficiency of the steaming apparatus. If the plank comes out of the box limber and a little too hot for bare hands, it is ready to put on the boat. If it seems just as stiff as when it went in and none too warm, it needs more steam. Bend the plank as quickly as you can, as thin planking loses heat rapidly. Work it gradually and evenly, and if hot it will give you no trouble.

Hot water and sacks, blankets, or large rags are a substitute for steaming used when there are not enough hard bends to warrant a steam box. Wrap the bending end of plank thickly with the sacks or what not. Have a large quantity of steaming hot water ready and a wash boiler half full is not too much. Saturate both sides with the hot water, but particularly the outer face of the plank; keep the whole hot by slowly pouring on the water until all the water is used. You can wait a little longer and then put on the plank. This method is a great aid in working a cold plank, but cannot compare with a steam box. Do not lay the plank flat on the bottom of the steam box but place a block under the end so that the steam will circulate all around it. The top of box is the hottest, and the open end should be plugged with rags or a sack.

Equipment Required By Law*

All motor-boats, whether propelled by inboard or outboard motor, are required by national law to carry certain equipment. The great majority of outboard boats and cruisers, also inboard and outboard runabouts and racers, are under twenty-six feet in length and therefore come under class one. The requirements for this class are briefly as follows:

Whistle.—To be capable of producing a blast prolonged for at least two seconds (usually a mouth whistle).

Lights.—Combination red-and-green lantern (or bow light and colored side lights) and stern light.

At anchor, a white light only, less than twenty feet above hull, and visible around the horizon for at least one mile.

Life Preservers.—One approved live preserver for each person on board, placed so as to be readily accessible. The buoyant cushion if of proper manufacture may count as a life preserver, but pneumatic appliances or those filled with ground cork are outlawed.

A fire extinguisher capable of extinguishing gasoline fires.

Choosing the Motor

In some instances the boat is built to suit the motor and in others the motor is chosen to fit the boat. It is with the later instance that we are here concerned. The most common error is to over-power the boat. Any hull can economically use just so much power; more than this amount will not produce results in keeping with the added expenditure. In fact, after a certain point is reached the power may be doubled and increase the speed of the boat less than one knot. Referring to the larger boat field for an example: a certain 35-footer, displacement 7.7 tons, has a speed of 8 knots with 25 H. P.; increasing this to 60 H. P. will realize less than an additional knot.

The planing boat, and particularly the step hydroplane, is an exception to the above. In the latter boat, after a certain point is reached the speed increases directly in proportion to the power expended. The vee-bottom runabout of proper design, while not as efficient as the hydro, should be considered a planing boat, and with the racing boat not limited as to power installed. The outboard association's rules govern the piston displacement in the racing craft as well as hull weight (see *Wasp,* an outboard racer).

As a suggestion in choosing a motor I have outlined the following, to be interpreted with quite a bit of latitude:

Motors up to 4 H. P.—Dinghys, canoes, and light rowboats and skiffs.

Motors 4 H. P. to 8 H. P.—Small runabouts, outboard open boats, heavy skiffs, and as a sailboat auxiliary.

8 H. P. to 16 H. P.—Large runabouts, outboard cruisers, and heavy open boats; also as a sailboat auxiliary.

Over 16 H. P.—Large runabouts and racing hulls.

*This information has not been updated and does not necessarily reflect current laws.

Building the Round-Bottom Boat

Starting with laying down the boat and with Fig. No. 1. There is, of course, no chine line, but otherwise there is little difference and the lines are faired up by use of waterlines and buttocks. Diagonals are often used, but for simplicity may be dispensed with here. The sawed frame, as in Figs. Nos. 5 and 6, is represented by a form, and these forms have centreline, sheerline, etc., marked on them in the same manner. The boat is erected just as in Fig. No. 9 or 10 except that there will be about half the number of forms. A larger number of ribbands are used, about five to each side or sufficient to pull the bent frames fair from sheer to rabbet. The frames are then bent much as described for *Vagabond;* nail squarely into them through the ribbands while hot; use bright or ungalvanized nails, and the whole ribband will pull off easily later on. The planking must be hollowed out with a round plane around the sharp curve of bilge; otherwise, there is little difference except that more care is necessary with the bevels.

Braces are nailed inside to help retain the shape, and the forms are removed. From this point on there is practically no difference in the construction of the two types of boat. Taking the illustrations not already mentioned, the forms are assembled in the same manner as in Fig. No. 5, except that they are not bevelled; rabbet is cut as in Figs. Nos. 7 and 8, garboard laid out as in Fig. No. 11; the caulking seam, butt blocks, beam camber are just as shown in the various other sketches and as described in text.

The Care of the Boat

A small boat requires a certain amount of attention if it is to be kept in proper shape. We have all seen a nicely built boat tied half-submerged to some mooring or hauled out in the open and unprotected from the rain or hot sun. It would seem that any one who has expended considerable energy and cash in building a boat would be willing to give it the slight amount of attention necessary to care for it properly.

Small boats should be in the water as little as practical. Punts, skiffs, and rowboats are easily hauled out, and should be high and dry when not in use. The larger boats are harder to handle and, of course, the cruiser or heavy sailboat cannot be hauled out except for winter storage, painting, or repairs. A runabout, racing outboard, or any other high-speed boat must not be handicapped by useless weight in the form of watersoaked planking if the best performance is required. Many owners of large runabouts install expensive lifting gear in their boat houses, and it will certainly pay the small-boat owner to obtain a few rollers and planking or other gear necessary for hauling out his boat.

Under the care of the boat should come varnishing, painting, and caulking, and these are covered under their respective headings. Properly cared for, however, a minimum of the above will be found necessary. When recaulking "reefe" out the old putty and if possible the old cotton. The point of a small flat file, bent at right angles and flattened to a point, makes a good tool for hooking out the old putty and cotton.

Tools

The amateur boatbuilder is generally mechanically inclined and possesses most of the tools needed in boatbuilding. A few additions however may be necessary, and whether one or two or a larger number are purchased they might as well be of the type or pattern most suited for the work.

They should not be of large or heavy pattern; choose a light hammer, also chisels; and a small finetooth saw is much better than a large coarse one. A rip-saw will be needed, and this is one place where size is an asset. A hand drill is very handy in drilling, and the type with the turning handle on the side is better than a push drill. A "hold on" may consist of a short stub of shafting, a maul head, or a heavy hammer. The matter of clamps is taken up under planking, and under bevels is mentioned a small bevel which is very useful.

If a small square is purchased the combination sliding tongue is better, as it can serve as a gauge as well. When selecting bits avoid the large worm, as it will often split the end of a plank before the bit itself starts to cut. The caulking iron for small boats comes almost to a sharp edge, and do not buy one with a thick blade end, as it is only suitable for large work.

Wooden planes are seldom available, though universally used for some work by the boatbuilder. A wood smoothing plane is much superior for smoothing off the hull, though, of course, an iron one will do, but makes harder work of it. A jack-plane or jointer is almost a necessity for fairing up plank edges on the bench, as a shorter one will leave a lumpy edge. There is a little tool called the "scriber," costing, I think, fifteen (15) cents, really a small compass, and indispensable for "scribing" or fitting throughout the boat. Nail punches should be heavy, as few finish nails are used.

If many screws are put in, a spiral screw-driver is handy, and buy one that has a spring in it. One large and a small chisel will suffice. In constructing some boats a rabbet plane is necessary, and a combination rabbet and smoother provides two tools in one.

Selecting a Design

Boats as a rule cannot be classed as easy to build. True, they have two sides and a bottom just as has a box, but here the resemblance ends. Seaworthiness, appearance, and utility mould into their form twists and curves found in no other construction.

Some judgment should be used in matching, building skill, and the plan chosen. The amateur boatbuilder is generally mechanically inclined and possesses considerable natural ability, also manual training in our schools has provided many with valuable experience in woodworking and, in some cases, actual boatbuilding experience. The more skillful should have little trouble with the most difficult of the designs shown here.

On the other hand, if wood-working experience is lacking, and the builder has little confidence in his ability, it would be wiser to tackle one of the simpler designs first. For a rowboat I would suggest a punt, pram, or small skiff; for an outboard boat the larger skiff shown here, also *Fisherman* or *Camper*. There are two very simple sailboats in *Truant* and *Flattee*. It is often possible to obtain a little professional help; an hour or two for a few evenings will help over the hard spots and at no great cost.

There is a saying to the effect that anything worth while cannot be accomplished without considerable effort, and this, of course, holds true in building a boat. There will be moments when you wished you had never started, but when it is all done and you are enjoying the fruit of your labor, just ask yourself: Which was the most fun, using it or building it?

Designs

Stubby—a nine-foot dinghy or rowboat that will carry four.

Takeapart—a light-weight punt that can be built either as a one or two-piece boat.

Two skiffs—from a proven model, one large and one small.

Camper and Fisherman—two rugged sixteen-foot outboard boats for fishing and camping.

Photo by Morris Rosenfeld

Sunbeam and Sunray—two modern outboard runabouts, large and small.

Marine—an attractive outboard cruiser with two berths and galley.

Wasp—an outboard racer for classes B to E and developed from successful boats.

Hornet—a 125 or 151 class hydroplane of modern trend.

Tern—an inboard runabout with forward-driving position.

Truant—a small sailboat of inexpensive construction.

Curlew—a fifteen-and-one-half-foot afternoon sailboat.

Flattee—"Ted" Geary's famous development-class racing sailboat.

Vagabond—a keel sloop with cruising accommodations, a real little ship.

The above designs are in no way experimental or untried, but are developed from proven models, with a careful effort for improvement where possible. There are sixteen boats shown, a sufficient number to roughly cover the small-boat field. The scope of these designs can be greatly broadened, as in most cases it is quite feasible to shorten or lengthen these boats within reasonable limits. In larger craft this would not be advisable, but in the small boat with its constantly varying loads and distribution of weight, a change in waterline length is not so vital.

Broadly speaking, and the planning boat excepted, resistance is decreased by lengthening a boat even though in doing so some weight is added, and the opposite holds true in shortening a hull. In changing one dimension and not the other, relative proportions are, of course, lost. It is comparatively easy to lengthen a design, but to widen it is a different matter. Roughly speaking, a change in length of over 10 per cent should not be considered, and even less would be advisable with such boats as *Hornet;* none at all in *Flattee* if you wish to engage in class competition.

To lengthen or shorten a design the frames or stations are merely spaced a little closer or farther apart. Take as an example the fourteen-foot eight-inch runabout *Sunbeam.* There are eight frame spaces of twenty-two inches each. By changing the spacing to twenty-one inches we shorten the boat to fourteen feet, and by making them twenty-three inches we lengthen the boat to fifteen feet four inches. This changes frame bevels slightly, also the stem rabbet and bearding line, but not enough but that it can be taken care of by a little trimming. This will not be necessary if the lines are completely laid down to the new length. The lumber order must, of course, be altered in respect to length of planking and fore-and-aft members.

The construction methods and description in this book will apply to almost any small-boat design, and are not written to cover the following designs only.

"Stubby," a Pram
Dinghy or Rowboat

THIS LITTLE BOAT is similar to one designed by the author for *Pacific Motorboat* and published in the February, 1930, issue of that magazine. It has proven quite popular and a large number have been built. This boat was 8′ 6″ long with a beam of 4′, carried four people nicely and made a light, seaworthy little tender or rowboat. The new design has been simplified somewhat, and has but one knuckle instead of two, and is a little longer being 9′ by 4′. In ease of construction, this type of boat is excelled only by the simple square-end punt, to which it is in every way superior.

The lumber order follows:

Side Plank—2 pcs. ½″ × 14″—10′ cedar or 4 pcs. ½″ × 8″ cedar and make use of the dory lap.
Bottom Plank—2 pcs. ½″ × 8″—9′, 4 pcs. ½″ × 8″—8′ cedar.
Transoms—Aft—1 pc. 1¹⁄₁₆″ × 16″—3′ 6″ or two narrower pieces glued. For'd 1 pc. 1¹⁄₁₆″ × 10″—2′ mahogany, spruce, etc.
Frames—9 B. M. ¾″ oak 4′ and up but not less than 8″ wide, also 1 pc. ½″ × 6″—2′ oak, for frame corners or gussets.
Seats or Thwarts—1 pc. ¾″ × 10″—4′, 1 pc. ¾″ × 10″—3′ and 1 pc. ½″ × 10″—8′ cedar.
Floor Boards—1 pc. ½″ × 6″—7′, 2 pcs. ½″ × 4″—7′ and 2 pcs. ½″ × 4″—5′ cedar.
Transom Knees and Breast Hook—1 pc. 2″ × 6″—3′ oak.
Seat Knees (optional)—1 pc. 1″ × 6″—2′ oak.
Guard—2 pcs. 1″ half-round 10′ hardwood.
Skeg—1 pc. 1¹⁄₁₆″ × 6″—4′, 1 pc. 1¹⁄₁₆″ × ¾″—5′.
Gunwale and Chine—4 pcs. ½″ × 1½″—9′ oak.
Seat Riser and Keel Batten from plank edgings.

You may substitute spruce for oak in the bottoms of frames for lightness, and make other changes as explained under "Boatbuilding Woods." No steam box is required.

The construction methods and details in the text of this book will apply closely here, and the following is intended to fill in the gaps and treat this craft individually.

The boat is set up and remains until planked, bottom side up much as in Fig. No. 9, except that the floor takes the place of the erecting stringer. Frames Nos. 2 and 4 are assembled as shown with sides extended 6″ and 7½″ respectively. The aft transom has a piece nailed on each side, as shown. All frame and transom bevels may be obtained closely enough from the drawing, using a small bevel.

In setting up, strike a straight line on the floor for a centreline. Lay out stations Nos. 2 and 4 square off it and 36″ apart. On each of these nail a 1″ × 4″ or 2″ × 4″ cleat, placing each on the midship side of the station lines. Frames Nos. 2 and 4 may now be set in place with ends on the floor and securely nailed against the cleats. Centre them to centreline on the floor by means of a two-foot square, also square them plumb fore and aft and brace in this position. The aft transom is next and the piece on the floor should have its aft edge 36½″ aft of station No. 4. The extra ½″ is to allow for rake, as shown. Fasten the ends of the transom cleats to the floor piece, centre it and brace it so that its top aft edge is 34″ from station No. 4 to give the specified rake of 2″, as shown. The for'd transom is left straight on top and this edge is bevelled so that it fits the floor when your square shows it at the proper rake of 6¼″, as per plan. The ½″ × 1½″ cleats shown on sides of transom are to receive some of the plank fastenings, also ends of chine piece, and should be fastened in place before they are set up.

The ½″ × 1½″ chine pieces are next, and fasten to each frame and transom with two 1½″ × No. 8 screws. The three intermediate frames follow, and as a guide in laying them out a ribband will have to be tacked along outside of frames at sheer mark, the gunwales will do. As all the frame floors have the same shape or rise of floor, the three floor pieces are cut to same shape as laid out for station No. 4. These I would fit in place, cutting them to fit between the chines and keeping their centres on the boat's

30

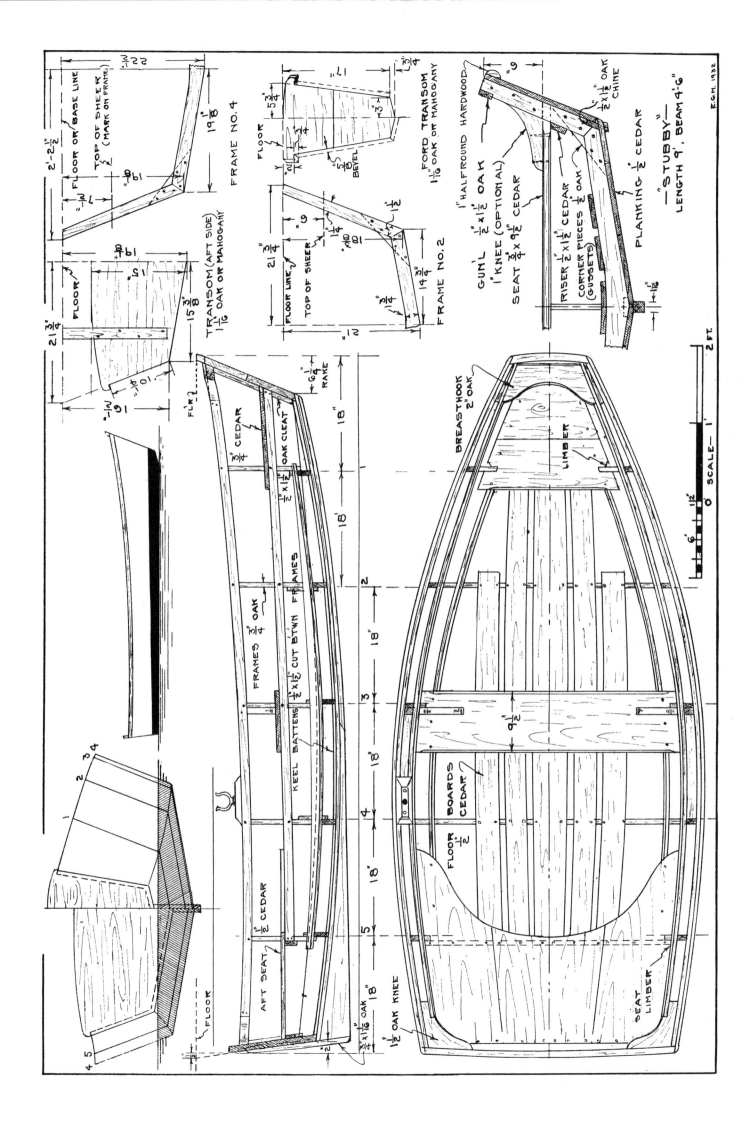

"STUBBY"
LENGTH 9', BEAM 4'-6"

E.G.M. 1932

SCALE — 1'

centreline. Tack them in place and fit and bevel the side pieces of the frames; these will lap the floors and are fastened to each with two 1½" No. 8 screws. After side pieces are fitted they should be marked on the floor piece and the whole frame removed and fastened on the bench. Before replacing frame No. 1 tack a brace or cross-band across near the top, as it will take quite a strain when the side plank is bent.

When the frames are all faired up you are ready for the side plank. The bottom of the plank will be practically straight and the width to sheerline at each frame may be laid off from this edge. If two planks are used on each side their edges should be joined by a one-inch dory lap, as shown in Fig. No. 18. In any case put a small thread of cotton on transom edges and start the plank by fastening it to the for'd transom and working aft. The bend is not excessive, but if the plank seems stiff and brittle make use of the hot-water-and-sack method explained under "Steaming Plank." Fasten to frames with 4d galvanized nails, use 6d in transom and fasten to chine with 1¼" copper boat nails clinched over chine on inside; also put marine glue between plank and chine.

The bottom planking should start at the centre and provide a ³⁄₃₂" caulking seam; lay cotton across transoms and all around edge of side plank. Fasten around outside to chine and plank edge, using 4d galvanized nails and at the tip or shim ends a few 1½" No. 6 screws. Plane a flat spot full length of centre seam for the skeg; caulk and putty the seam and put on the skeg. It may be fastened to each frame except No. 5 with large galvanized nails and to transom with the ¾" × 1¹⁄₁₆" oak strip.

The boat may now be turned over and the ½" × 1½" keel battens fitted between the frames and to bevel of bottom. Fasten them through into skeg with 6d galvanized nails. The seat riser is next and then the seats; the seat limbers shown may seem unusual but if you have ever tried to drain out all the water by turning a boat on its side you will appreciate their practicability. The little one-inch thwart knees are optional, but I think well worth while. Fit them in place before the centre seat is fastened and then remove seat and screw-fasten them through the seat. The gunwale may be riveted through frames and planking with copper rivets, as described for *Fisherman*, or else screw-fastened. The balance of the job needs no special mention.

An Eight-Foot Punt

THIS IS THE simplest of craft and may be built as a takeapart fishing and hunting boat or as an out and out one-piece punt. In two pieces it may be easily stowed for transportation, and being very light is suitable for "packing in" to inaccessible fishing and hunting grounds. Built according to plans, the assembled boat should weigh about seventy pounds, or about thirty-five pounds per section, the aft piece being a little the heavier. Constructed as a one-piece boat, the centre division pieces are omitted and the deep floor is moved one frame aft to centre of boat. The centre seat is in about the right position for rowing, and oarlocks may be fitted just aft of it for that purpose. The boat would then serve as a light and simple yacht tender or ferry, but it must be remembered that these craft are notoriously wet in rough water and poor sea boats.

The Lumber Order

Sides—2 pcs. ³⁄₈″ × 14″—8′ or 2 pcs. 6″ and 2 pcs. 8″ wide.

Transoms—1 pc. ¾″ × 14″—3′ and 1 pc. ¾″ × 16″—2′ 6″ (for'd).

Bulkheads—1 pc. ¾″ × 12″—7′ or 1 pc. ¾″ × 14″—7′ (see text).

Bottom—1 pc. ¼″ × 36″—4′, 1 pc. ¼″ × 36″—3′ 6″ W. P. plywood or 30 B. M. ³⁄₈″ × 7½″ cedar.

Frames—1 pc. ⁵⁄₈″ × 6″—8′ or 30 Lin. ⁵⁄₈″ × 1½″.

Chine—2 pcs. ½″ × 1″—8′.

Floor Boards—7 pcs. ½″ × 3″—3′, 2 pcs. ½″ × 1½″—8′ battens.

Deep Floors—2 pcs. ½″ × 6″—3′.

Skeg—1 pc. ¾″ × 4″—4′.

Seats—2 pcs. ½″ × 10″—8′.

Outer Corner Batten—2 pcs. ³⁄₈″ × 1″—8′.

Guards—2 pcs. ½″ × 1¼″—8′.

In the above order the scantlings are quite light to keep weight at the minimum. Built as a one-piece boat, weight will probably be not so vital and the scantlings may be increased to advantage. The sides should be ½″ thick and

bottom increased to ³⁄₈″ plywood, or ½″ lumber and transoms to ⅞″. No steaming is required.

The construction methods and details in the text of this book will apply closely here, and the following is intended to fill in the gaps and treat this craft individually.

It might be well to mention that in this, or in any other light construction, waterproof glue should be used wherever feasible, as it will greatly increase the strength of the boat.

The two side pieces are first cut to shape and the chine battens fastened to them; mark but do not cut for'd end of side plank. Use 1″ copper boat nails clinched on inside and glue between. Cut each end of chine to fit against inside edge of transom, as shown, and allow bottom edge to project ⅛″ below side board all along, to allow for bevelling later. The frames are then fitted and fastened, using 2d and 3d galvanized nails; omit for present the frames at bulkheads and transoms. The latter are now sawed to shape and mark centreline on each; the bulkheads will require no bevel and transom bevels can be closely obtained from the drawings, using a small bevel. At top and outer edges of each bulkhead there must be glued and fastened a wedge-shaped piece, as shown in plan, if 12″ lumber is used to bring this edge a half inch or so above top of side board. The frame pieces, including bottom pieces, are fastened to the bulkheads, using 1¼″ No. 8 screws. Notch out of both bulkhead and frame pieces for chine; as the latter is continuous and should fit snugly here for a watertight job, try a short piece in the notch to be sure of a good fit. The bulkheads are placed back to back, as in drawing, and separated by heavy strips of cardboard, so that your saw may be slipped between when boat is cut in two later.

Tack aft transom in place between the side boards and next the centre bulkheads; now place a rope around for'd ends of plank and pull them together and fasten for'd transom. (See *Fisherman.*) Tack a straight edge across top or bottom from transom to transom and square up the ship from this and brace across corners. A word about fastening transoms. If the nails are first driven through a piece of ³⁄₈″ scrap any discrepancy in bevel may be remedied by loosening the fastenings and remedying the defect. If none exists, the piece is split away and fastenings driven home. Use 4d galvanized nails here, as in the end grain they are as good as screws. A few saw cuts may be necessary between ends of chines and transom to insure a snug fit. Put thick glue between bulkhead and transom ends and the plank. Transom frames, including bottom pieces, may now be fitted and fastened in same manner as the frames on the bulkheads, also fastened to planking. As the bulkheads will be the point of connection between the two halves, the planks must be particularly well fastened here, so use 1″ No. 6 screws into bulkhead and bulkhead frame, spacing them about one and one-half inches apart. Nails will do in transoms.

The two deep floors are next and will have to be fitted against frame sides, on account of the slight bevel here (screw-fasten). The ½″ × 1½″ bottom battens run from bulkhead to transoms, but do not cut through any of them, but notch into the deep floors and transom and bulkhead frame pieces. The bottom is faired up and the plywood bottom fitted, fasten with 1″ No. 6 screws placed about ten to the foot across transom and bulkheads and 3d galvanized nails along sides and across deep floors; use thick glue all around. Fasten into the ½″ × 1½″ bottom battens with 1″ copper boat nails, clinched. If plywood is not available use ⅜″ cedar and provide a ¹⁄₁₆″ caulking seam. Plank athwartship, and as the material is thicker, slightly fewer fastenings will be required; use 1¼″ screws instead of 1″.

The skeg is fastened from inside, using 1″ No. 6 screws through bottom; screw-fasten from outside into bulkheads, deep floors, and ends. The for'd seat is permanent and also the outer boards of the others, as they help to stiffen the boat. The inner sections serve as lids for the lockers. Drill the ⁷⁄₁₆″ holes shown for connecting bolts, which should be ⅜″ diameter galvanized machine bolts, and rubber gaskets will be required for lower holes. Tack gaskets in place and use washers at both ends of all bolts.

In bulkhead corners are shown metal clips or angles; these may be cut from a 1½″ × 1½″ angle iron or bent from a ⅛″ × 1″ iron or brass strip. If of angles, cut to 1½″ lengths in order to obtain two fastenings in each web. If of bent clips, make long arm against sides, as shown. Use ³⁄₁₆″ brass bolts through guard and bulkhead. This, of course, after boat is cut in two. The floor boards are placed as shown to relieve the strain on the thin bottom. Fasten the ⅜″ × 1″ oak chafing strips to the chine and side plank, using 1½″ No. 8 screws spaced about three inches. The strips well fastened will doubly secure the bottom to side plank. After guards are fastened (and, by the way, use glue under them), the boat may be sawed in two.

In case 14″ lumber is used for bulkheads allow the extra 2½″ to project above the layout dimensions which are for 11½″ lumber. As mentioned in text it is very important that you paint the plywood thoroughly, particularly the edges.

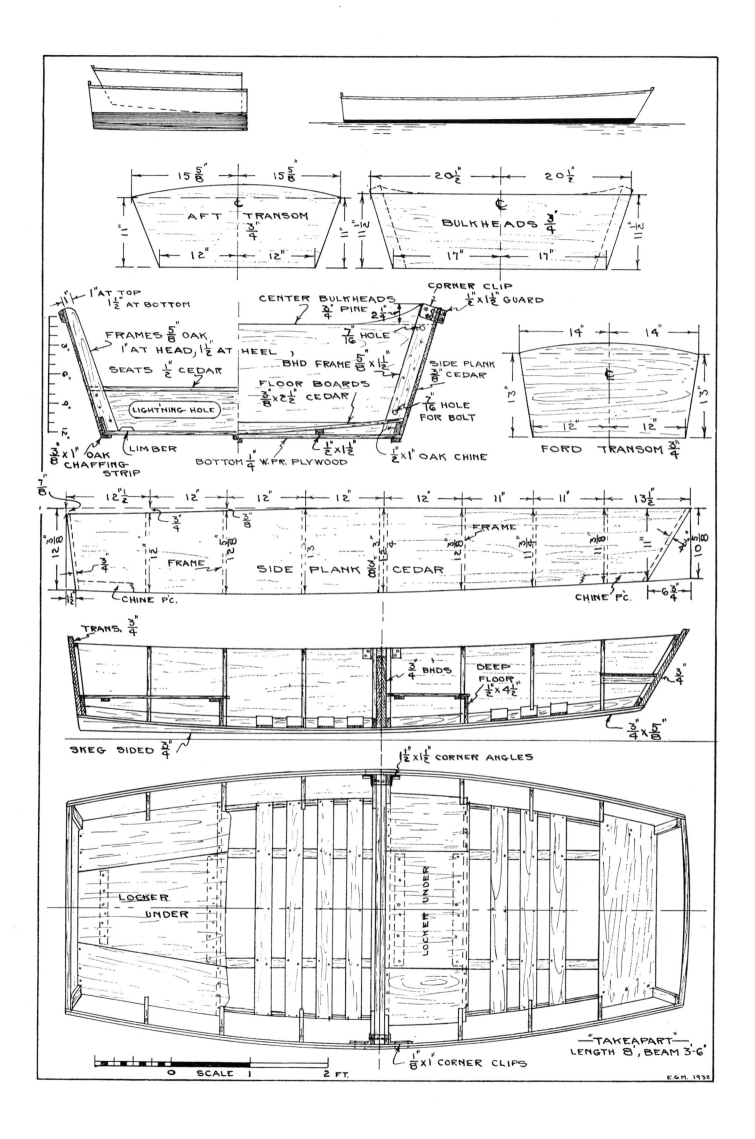

15⅝" | 15⅝"

AFT TRANSOM ¾"

1" | 1"
12" | 12"

20½" | 20½"

BULKHEADS ¾"

1½" | 1½"
17" | 17"

1" AT TOP
1½ AT BOTTOM

CENTER BULKHEADS ¾" PINE
CORNER CLIP
1½"×1½" GUARD

2¾"

FRAMES ⅝" OAK
1" AT HEAD, 1½ AT HEEL

SEATS ½" CEDAR

BHD FRAME ⅝"×1½"

FLOOR BOARDS
⅜"×2½" CEDAR

SIDE PLANK
⅜" CEDAR

7/16" HOLE

7/16" HOLE
FOR BOLT

LIGHTNING HOLE

⅜"×1" OAK
CHAFFING
STRIP

LIMBER

BOTTOM ¼" W.PR. PLYWOOD

½"×1½"

½"×1" OAK CHINE

14" | 14"

13" | 13"

FORD TRANSOM ¾"

12" | 12"

⅞"

12½" | 12" | 12" | 12" | 12" | 11" | 11" | 13½"

12⅜"

¾" | ⅝" |
FRAME | ¾" |
FRAME

SIDE PLANK CEDAR

10⅝"

½"
CHINE P'C.

CHINE P'C.

6¾"

TRANS. ¾"

¾" BHDS

DEEP
FLOOR
1½"×4½"

¾"

¾"×⅝"

SKEG SIDED ¾"

1½"×1½" CORNER ANGLES

LOCKER

UNDER

LOCKER UNDER

⅛"×1" CORNER CLIPS

"TAKEAPART"
LENGTH 8', BEAM 3'-6"

0   SCALE 1   2 FT.

E.G.M. 1932

Two Skiffs

THE LOWLY SKIFF might well be called the universal boat. Its simple and inexpensive construction are its strong points, and these are exceeded only in the punt, a much inferior craft, almost useless in rough water. It is a strange paradox that plans of them are as scarce as the boats are numerous. Although "how to builds" have been published of hundreds of other craft, it is hard to recall one of a single skiff.

The two shown here are from a proven model, easy to "pull" and a good rough-water craft, as skiffs go. The smaller one is eleven feet six inches long by three feet ten inches beam and intended to serve where a light, easily handled boat is desired, either as a yacht tender or for summer camp, where it must be frequently carried up and down the beach. The larger boat is fourteen feet six inches by four feet five inches, and though a light boat its size limits its portability, but it should make an ideal outboard boat. Both are of ample freeboard and beam, which, combined with the raking stem, should make them seaworthy and dry. The gunwale and the seat or thwart knees are refinements which are sometimes omitted, and may be in this case. It is not necessary to steam the planking.

The illustration shows the general shape of the boat, also the gunwales, seat risers, stern seat, transom knees, and the cleats on the transom for an outboard motor.

Lumber Order for 11' 6" Skiff

Stem—1 pc. 1¾" × 6"—3' and 1 pc. 1½" × 3"—3'.
Frames—45 lineal ¾" × 2" if metal corners are used or if not 30 lineal ¾" × 2"— bottom and 10 lineal ¾" × 6"—sides.
Side Planks—2 pcs. ½" × 10"—12' and 2 pcs. ½" × 12"—12'.
Bottom Plank—2 pcs. ½" × 10"—10' and 2 pcs. ½" × 10"—9'.
Gunwale, Guards and Seat Riser—4 pcs. ½" × 1½"—12' and 2 pcs. 9'.
Seats—1 pc. ¾" × 10"—8', 1 pc. ½" × 12"—4' and 1 pc. ½" × 8"—3'.

Floor Boards—4 pcs. ½" × 4"—8' and 2 pcs. ½" × 4"—6'.
Knees and Breasthook—1 pc. 1¾" × 8"—2' and 1 pc. 1" × 6"—3'.
Skeg and Shoe—1 pc. 1" × 4"—4' and 1 pc. 1" × ¾"—10'.
Transom—1 pc. 1¹⁄₁₆" × 15"—3' 1" (or 2 pcs. glued).

Lumber Order for 14' 6" Skiff

Stem—1 pc. 1¾" × 6"—3' 2" and 1 pc. 1½" × 3"—3'.
Frames—55 lineal ¾" × 2" if metal corners are used, or if not 33 lineal ¾" × 2"—bottom and 12 lineal ¾" × 6"—sides.
Side Plank—2 pcs. ½" × 12"—14' and 2 pcs. ½" × 12"—15'.
Bottom Plank—2 pcs. ½" × 10" N.—13' and 2 pcs. ½" × 10" N.—12'.
Gunwale, Guards and Seat Riser—2 pcs. ½" × 1½"—12' and 2 pcs. 14' and 2 pcs. 15'.
Seats—1 pc. ¾" × 10"—11' and 1 pc. ½" × 10"—8'.
Floor Boards—2 pcs. ½" × 4"—11', 2 pcs. ½" × 4"—10', and 2 pcs. ½" × 4"—9'.
Skeg and Shoe—1 pc. 1" × 6"—6' and 1 pc. ¾" × 1"—13'.
Transom—1 pc. 1¹⁄₁₆" × 16" N.—3' 6".
Knees and Breasthook—same as 11' 6" boat.

The construction methods and details in the text of this book will apply closely here, and the following is intended to fill in the gaps and treat this craft individually.

The frame and transom offsets are in this case to inside of planking, and these members are assembled to these lines. Lay out to full size stations Nos. 2 and 4 and transom and put together much as in Fig. No. 6 except that the cross-band is just a brace cut off flush with outer edge of frame. The left-hand side of midsection shows a metal clip in frame corner; this is generally employed in the boat shop, also is universal in dory construction. As the frame angle throughout varies but slightly, all clips are cut from the same pattern and are of about No. 16 gauge galvanized iron, are through-riveted, and purposely made ⅛″ or so scant around outer edge to avoid trimming. This method is better adapted to quantity production, and unless one has a leaning toward metal working I would advise following the construction shown on right-hand side of midsection. In this case all side frames are cut from same pattern; hold inboard edge against plank edge and by slipping one by the other they may all be cut from the 6″ lumber ordered and will have grain in best direction. Frame bevels may be obtained closely from the plan with a small bevel. Bevel side pieces only.

In stem detail the side angle or bevel is given instead of a dimension, as this permits the use of slightly thicker or thinner material. Do not cut this bevel above "top of side plank," but stop a half-inch short of this mark and trim off later when you fit the upper side plank.

The side planks are cut out as per layout dimensions and a 1″ dory lap planed on their joining edges. (See "Dory Lap.") Mark but do not trim aft ends until transom is fastened. The lower planks are nailed on each side of stem and a rope is passed around aft ends to pull them together. Frame No. 2 is fastened in place as the ends are drawn together and then No. 4 and the transom. A thin thread of cotton and thick paint should be placed on transom edge and stem side in lieu of caulking; also a 1″ × 2″ cleat screw-fastened across aft end of planks will prevent splitting. (See *Truant*.) Fasten to frames with 4d galvanized wire nails and to stem. Use 6d nails in transom and in stem if it is of soft wood. The top plank is now put on in much the same manner.

The balance of the frames come next. I would fit the bottom piece first and tack it in place, then fit and bevel the side pieces; mark them and remove the entire frame and fasten together on the bench. The ¾″ × 2″ intermediate floors are end-fastened to the side plank using 6d galvanized nails. The bottom is now planed fair, the limbers cut, and the bottom planked. Start at centre and provide a 1/16″

caulking seam, lay cotton around edges of side plank and transom. (See "Caulking.") Fasten in same manner as side plank and use 4d galvanized nails or 1½″ No. 8 screws into side plank, space about three inches, and wherever possible fasten outer edge into bottom frame rather than into side plank. The skeg and shoe may be put on now or later; in any case the centre seam must first be caulked and puttied and also painted. Where not too deep fasten skeg into frames, using long galvanized nails, the hardwood shoe is nailed into frames and skeg. A few nails should also be driven into the latter through plank from inside. The plank ends are flattened off to a 1½″ face and the face piece fitted and nailed into stem, using 16d galvanized nails.

Turning the boat over, the seat risers are put in and the seats, excepting the aft one. A one-inch thwart knee is shown in midsection, and if put in they will add to the strength and appearance of the boat, but are optional with the builder; if used see *Fisherman* text matter. Transom knees should be flush with top of transom and screw-fasten through into knee, using 2″ No. 12 screws; nail through plank into knee. The gunwales are shown let into frames one-fourth of an inch and may be screw-fastened or else tacked and through-riveted later, as explained under *Fisherman*. Their for'd ends are bevelled to fit stem side and a wedge-shaped piece fitted where shown to provide solid wood for fastening breasthook. The latter is ordered ¼″ thick to allow for a little crown or round on top, screw-fasten through plank into it, using 2½″ No. 12 screws. Floor boards and back seat finish the inside, but should not be fastened until the interior has been given two coats of paint.

Screw-fasten the oarlock blocks, as nails will eventually work loose if much rowing is done. The ring bolt into stem is for the painter. Have you ever turned a skiff on edge to drain it and found that the water would not run out from under the back seat? Limbers are shown cut just aft of the last frame and will effectively drain out this water; a corner trimmed off the seat here will provide the limber.

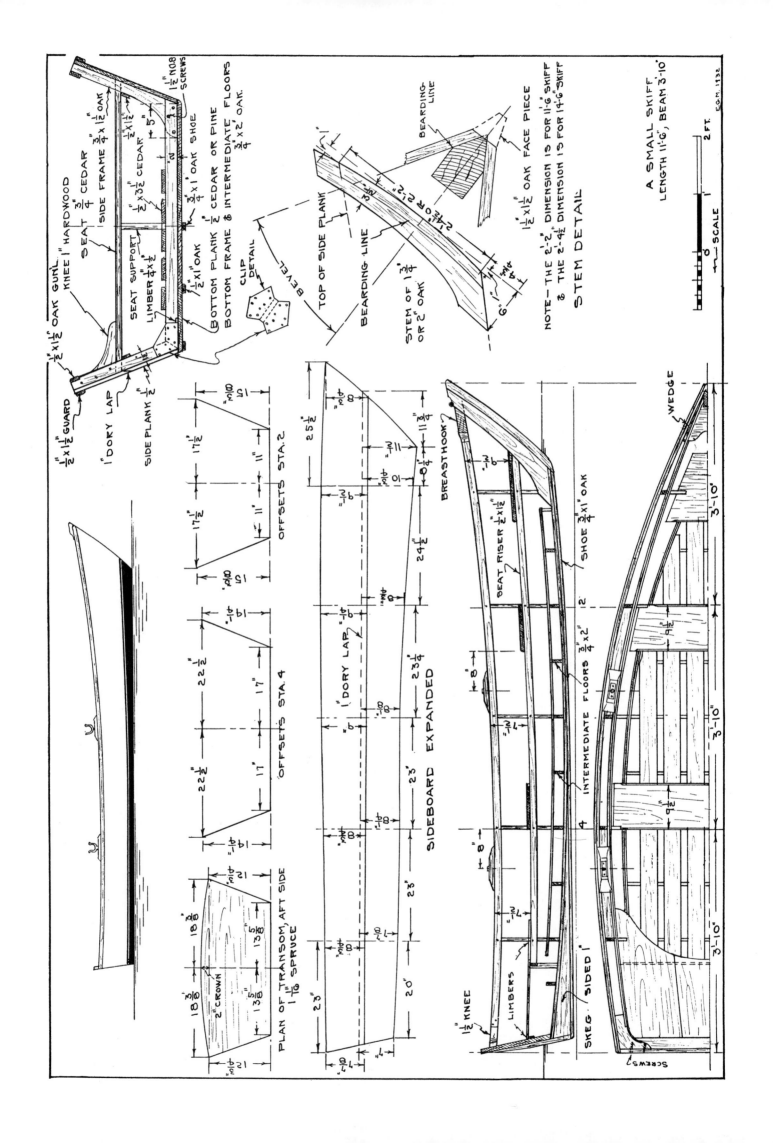

A SMALL SKIFF
LENGTH 11'-6", BEAM 3'-10"

STEM DETAIL

NOTE— THE 2'-2" DIMENSION IS FOR 11'-6 SKIFF
& THE 2'-4½" DIMENSION IS FOR 14'-6 SKIFF

OFFSETS STA. 2

OFFSETS STA. 4

PLAN OF TRANSOM, AFT SIDE
1⅛ SPRUCE

SIDEBOARD EXPANDED

SCALE

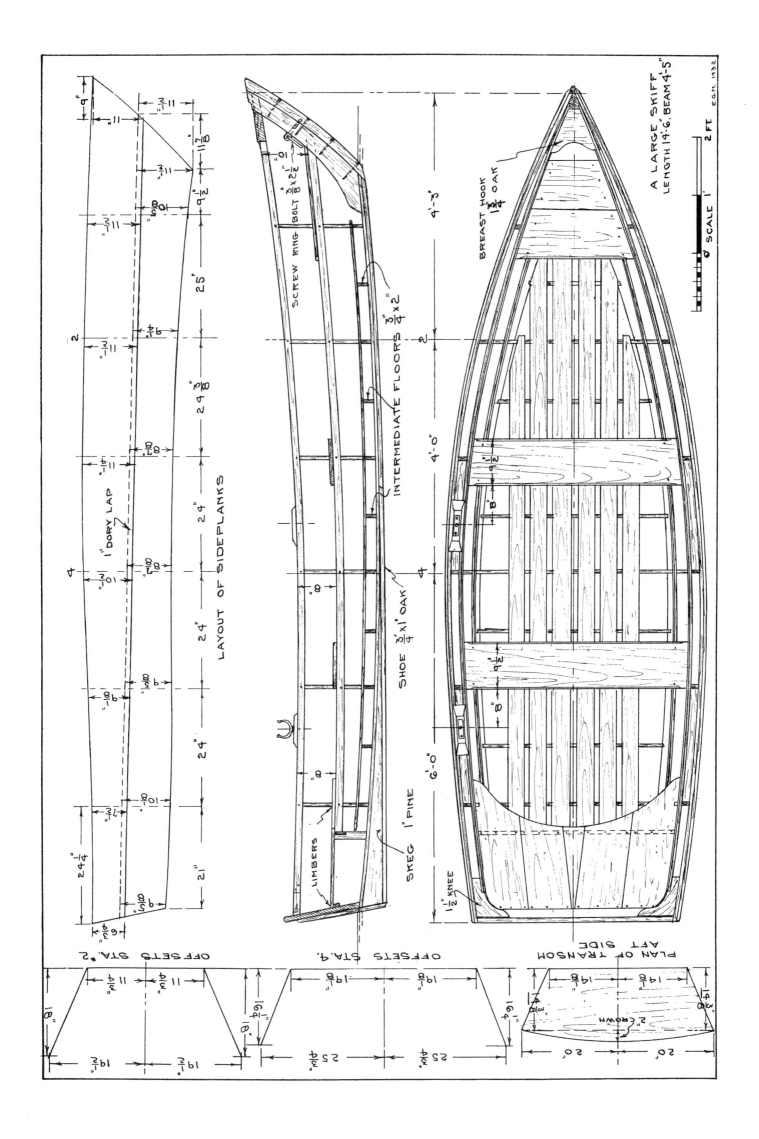

A LARGE SKIFF
LENGTH 14'-6", BEAM 4'-5"

E.G.H. 1932

SCALE 1"   2 FT.

BREAST HOOK
1¾ OAK

LAYOUT OF SIDEPLANKS

1" DORY LAP

SCREW RING BOLT 5/8 × 2½"

INTERMEDIATE FLOORS 3/4" × 2

SHOE 3/4" × 1" OAK

SKEG 1" PINE

LIMBERS

1½" KNEE

2" CROWN

PLAN OF TRANSOM   AFT SIDE

OFFSETS STA. 4.

OFFSETS STA. 2

"Camper"
and "Fisherman"

SHOWING INTERIOR CONSTRUCTION

HERE ARE TWO rugged, seaworthy, outboard boats, each approximately sixteen feet long with a beam of five feet. *Fisherman* is intended for what the name implies, and, fitted with an outboard motor, is suited for a long run to the fishing grounds in open water, where a good seaworthy boat is required. *Camper* is the same boat with a raised sheer and a deck forward, and is more an out-and-out outboard boat. It is designed to accommodate two or three on camping voyages; blankets, cooking gear, etc., may be stowed under the deck. A small anchor and rope locker is reached through the hatch forward, and a grab rail and toe rail make it accessible in rough water.

The hull shape is very similar to the round-bottom boat, and has proven very satisfactory in several of the author's "How to Build" designs, being easily propelled and possessing excellent heavy-weather qualities. The illustration is of one of these, and shows the hull shape; also most of the interior construction. It is not much more difficult to construct than the orthodox flat-bottomed skiff and is in every way superior to it.

No steam box is required, as there is no twist and the bends are not hard. If any difficulty is encountered, make use of hot water, as described under "Steaming."

Lumber Order for *Fisherman*

Stem—1 pc. 1¾" × 10"—4' and 1 pc. 1¼" × 4"—2' 6"—face.
Skeg—1 pc. 1¹⁄₁₆" × 8"—8'.
Transom—1 pc. 1¹⁄₁₆" × 12"—4' and 1 pc. 1¹⁄₁₆" × 10"—4'.
Frames—16 B. M. ¾" × 6" and wider, 5' long and up.
Planking—Bottom—2 pcs. ⁹⁄₁₆" × 10"—15', 2 pcs. ⁹⁄₁₆" × 10"—14', and 2 pcs. ⁹⁄₁₆" × 8"—12'.
Planking—Bilge—2 pcs. ⁹⁄₁₆" × 14" N.—16' or 4 pcs. ⁹⁄₁₆" × 8"—16'.
Planking—Topsides—2 pc. ⁹⁄₁₆" × 12"—17'.
Chine—2 pcs. ¾" × 1¾"—16'.
Seat Riser and Gunwale—4 pcs. ½" × 1½"—16'.
Seats—2 pcs. ⅞" × 10"—5' centre, 1 pc. ⅞" × 10"—3' forward. 2 pcs. ½" × 12"—6' and 1 pc. ½" × 12"—2' aft.

Transom Knees and Breasthook—1 pc. 1¾" × 8"—3'.
Thwart Knees—1 pc. 1" × 6"—3'.
Floor Boards—1 pc. ½" × 6"—12', 2 pcs. ½" × 4"—12'. 2 pcs. ½" × 4"—10' and 2 pcs. ½" × 4"—8'.
Chafing Strips—2 pcs. ½" × 1"—14', 2 pcs. 12' and 2 pcs. 8'.
Guards—2 pcs. 1¼" half round 17'.

Lumber Order For *Camper*

Skeg, transom, bottom and bilge plank, chafing strips, chine, stem, aft seat and transom knees same as above.

Frames—18 B. M. ¾" × 6" and wider—5' long and up.
Topsides Plank—2 pcs. ½" × 6"—17' and 2 pcs. ½" × 10"—17'.
Clamp—2 pcs. ½" × 3½"—16'.
Beams—1 pc. ¾" × 12"—8'.
Decking—30 B. M. ½" × 3" cedar T. and G.
Covering Board—1 pc. ½" × 10"—10'.
Floor Boards—1 pc. ½" × 6"—11', 2 pcs. ½" × 4"—11' and 2 pcs. ½" × 4"—10'.
Seats—1 pc. ⅞" × 10"—5'—centre and 1 pc. ⅞" × 14"—6'—sides.
Bulkhead—1 pc. ⅜" × 16"—4' plywood.
Guard—2 pcs. 1" halfround 8'—for'd and 2 pcs. 6'—aft.
Toe Rail and Grab Rail—1 pc. ¾" × 6"—6' and 1 pc. 1¾" × 1½"—4'.
Stem Face—1 pc. 1¼" × 6"—3'.

The construction methods and details in the text of this book will apply closely here, and the following is intended to fill in the gaps and treat this craft individually.

Both of these boats are laid down from the lines of *Fisherman*. The process of lofting is explained elsewhere and the boat may be laid down in full or just the body plan. In case you are constructing the raised deck boat just extend each frame up four or five inches on the body plan, and mark the new sheer heights from the offsets shown in upper left-hand corner; also allow about six inches more length on top of stem and crown transom, same as deck beams, with top edge ½″ above sheer, so that covering board will let in flush.

The frames are assembled just as in Fig. No. 6, and the boat is set up as in Fig. No. 9. Put cross-bands on frames Nos. 1, 2, 4, and 6, with top edge on setup line as shown in Fig. No. 6. The construction stringers should be placed thirty-six inches apart, as in lines drawings. The transom and frames No. 1, 2, 4, and 6 are set up, and the stem last. The keel batten and chine are next and notch into frames as shown. If chine is roughly bevelled on the bench it will be easier to bend; also it may be reduced to ½″ at stem. Fasten both to each frame with one 1½″ No. 10 screw, the forward end of chine fits against and fastens to side of stem. The balance of the frames are now fitted in place, and a ribband should be run close to the sheer mark on each side to hold them in place at this point. An extra or "cant" frame is shown for'd of frame one; its shape can now be obtained; it should fit against stem side below and fastens to it.

The bilge plank is first and requires considerable shaping; from the skeleton model I have made there will be about five inches convex curve in its top edge (next to top knuckle); the exact shape should be obtained by a spilling batten. (See "Planking.") A 1″ dory lap is planed on its outer face, as per plan. The bottom edge may be left full and planed off after fastening. If two narrow planks are substituted for one wide one, follow the same procedure as outlined for the bilge plank on *Curlew*. However, a 14″ width should not be hard to obtain and will save labor. Fasten plank to frames with 4d galvanized wire nails, using 6d in transom and stem. Use 1½″ copper boat nails spaced about three inches into chine and clinch, or else 1″ brass screws.

Start the bottom with the two centre planks and work out to each edge. As these planks are caulked provide a seam; and on edges of side plank and transom place a thread of cotton laid in thick paint (see "Caulking"), fasten into chine with 4d galvanized nails, or better still 1¼″ No. 8 screws. Fasten edges of centre plank to keel batten with 1¼″ copper boat nails clinched.

As this is best time to put on skeg, plane a flat spot about 1¹⁄₁₆″ wide down the centre seam, caulk and putty it and fit skeg. Fasten it into each frame with a large galvanized nail, but before skeg is fastened in place the plank ends for'd should be flattened off to provide for the stem face piece, which will be about 1¼″ wide; this would be difficult to do later.

The boat may now be turned right side up and the topside planked. There is little shaping to this plank and it should go on easily. In the lines of *Curlew* is detailed at several frames and at stem the change in shape of the 1″ lap on lower edge of this plank (also see *Curlew* text, and "The Dory Lap"). Leave fastenings out of top edge of plank for present, to be through-fastened with rivet shown later on.

From this point we will follow the construction of *Fisherman* and take up *Camper* later. The seat riser is fastened to frames with 4d galvanized nails and the seats fitted. The 1″ knees are of hardwood. They should be fitted before seat is fastened, marked on seat, which is removed, and the knee screw-fastened from under side of seat and the whole replaced. Screw-fasten through plank into knee and fasten through frames into knees with 4d galvanized nails. Limbers should be left at outer edge of back seat against transom and against frame so that all water will drain out when boat is turned on edge.

The transom knees are screw-fastened through transom and plank. The gunwales are next and a very neat way to fasten them is to drill through plank, frame, and gunwale and drive from outside an 8d or 10d copper nail; drive a tight-fitting copper burr over the point, cut off and rivet. Screw-fastening will make just as strong a job with less labor, but is not quite as shipshape. A wedge-shaped piece is fitted between gunwale and plank forward and the breasthook fastened through plank and all with 3″ No. 14 screws. The stem face piece is screw-fastened into stem with screw heads well countersunk so that profile of stem and keel may be faired to suit the eye. Guard, floor boards, chafing strips, and other odds and ends will finish the job. The long chafing strips are for inside, the short for outer edge of bottom.

Continuing with Construction of *Camper*

The first or lower topside plank should now be put on; use the 6″ plank. A dory lap is first worked on its top edge, the fitting of bottom edge is covered in *Fisherman*. Clamp and beams are now put in, as explained under "Deck Beams, Shelf, and Clamp." Before this can be done, however, the bulkhead filler shown on aft side of frame No. 3 and the 1″ seat knee will have to be fitted; the latter entails putting in seat riser and centre seat, as explained in the former boat, as is also the fastening of transom knee. 4d galvanized nails will suffice to fasten clamp to frames, being careful not to split them when fastening near the top.

The bulkhead on frame No. 3 is fastened to beam and to frame and filler with 3d galvanized nails. The last plank is put on and top faired up ready for the deck and covering board. A wedge-shaped piece will be needed to fill in above clamp aft of bulkhead, as shown.

The cleat filler and the low bulkhead at frame No. 1 should be fitted, the inside of boat painted, and the deck laid; fasten deck with 4d galvanized nails. Fasten the covering board to clamp and plank and to filler with 1¼″ No. 8 screws; also to knee and transom. The deck canvas turns down all around and is covered by guards and by the ³⁄₈″ × 1″ bulkhead facer; where it crosses covering board just fold under and fasten down with a row of tacks. A plain 1″ coaming or frame is fastened around the for'd hatch; the crown of deck will reduce the end pieces to about ⁵⁄₈″ in height at centre. A good method for battening down the hatch cover is to run a light line (shown by dotted line) from centre of cover through a hole in the bulkhead, back to a convenient cleat in cockpit. The line remains rove at all times and is loosened to remove hatch cover. The little swash strip is best screw-fastened from below. Mark each side of strip on deck and drill holes through deck, replace and fasten. Fasten toe rail into beams and plank edge, using 1½″ No. 8 screws. On outboard profile is shown a guard aft at knuckle line; it should be tapered at forward end and is screw-fastened to frames and to planking between.

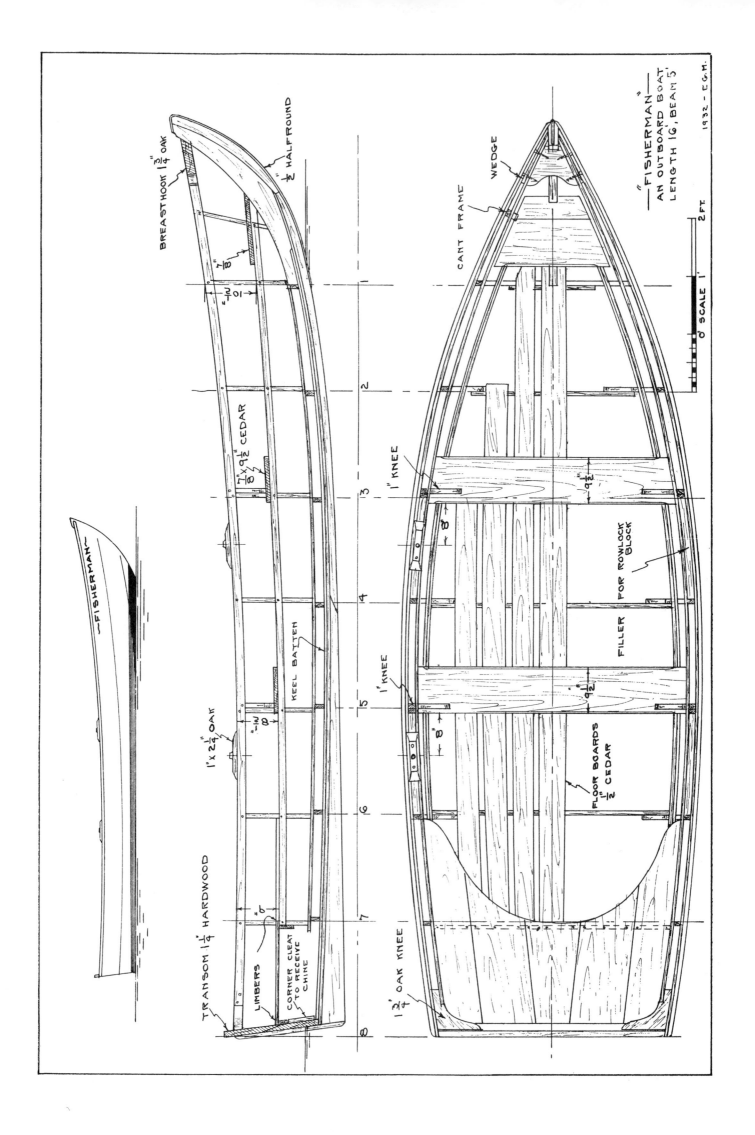

"FISHERMAN"
AN OUTBOARD BOAT
LENGTH 16', BEAM 5'

1932 - E.G.M.

0'   SCALE 1'   2 FT.

BREASTHOOK 1¾" OAK

½" HALFROUND

10½"

⅞"

⅞" x 9½" CEDAR

KEEL BATTEN

1" x 2¼" OAK

8"
⅛"

TRANSOM 1¼" HARDWOOD

6"

LIMBERS

CORNER CLEAT TO RECEIVE CHINE

~FISHERMAN~

CANT FRAME

WEDGE

1" KNEE

9½"

8"

FILLER FOR ROWLOCK BLOCK

FILLER

1" KNEE

9½"

8"

FLOOR BOARDS ½" CEDAR

1¾" OAK KNEE

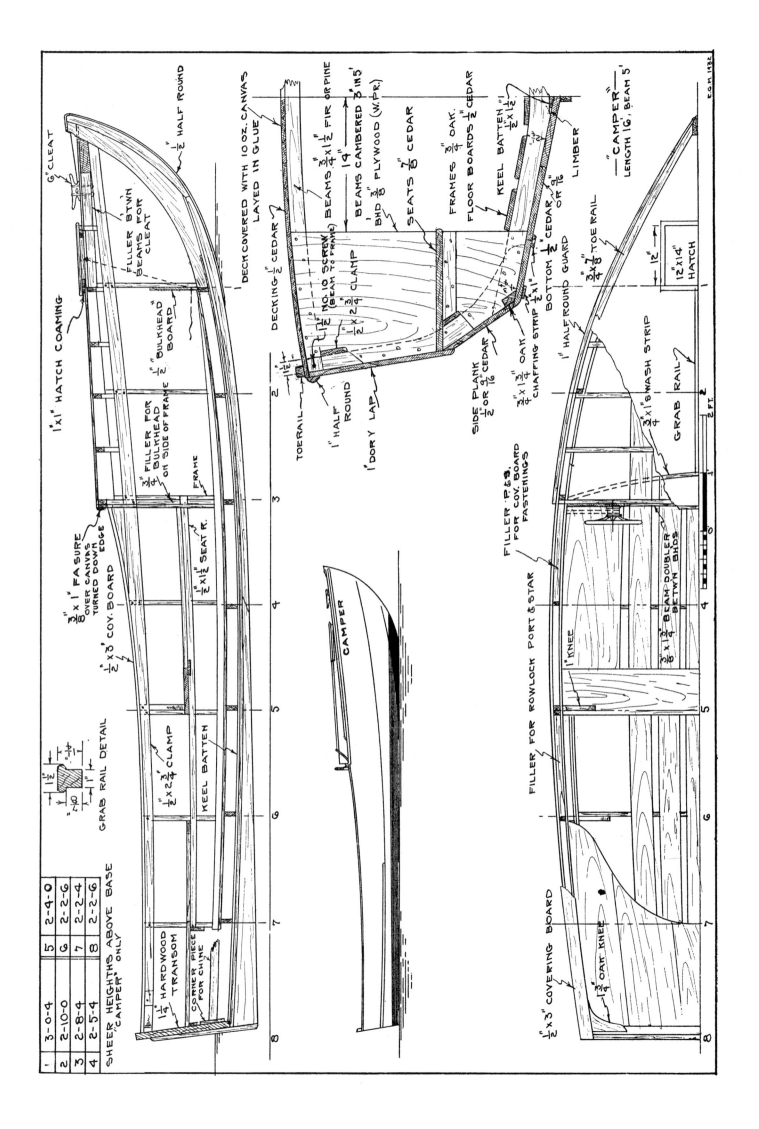

"CAMPER"
LENGTH 16', BEAM 5'

E.G.M. 1432

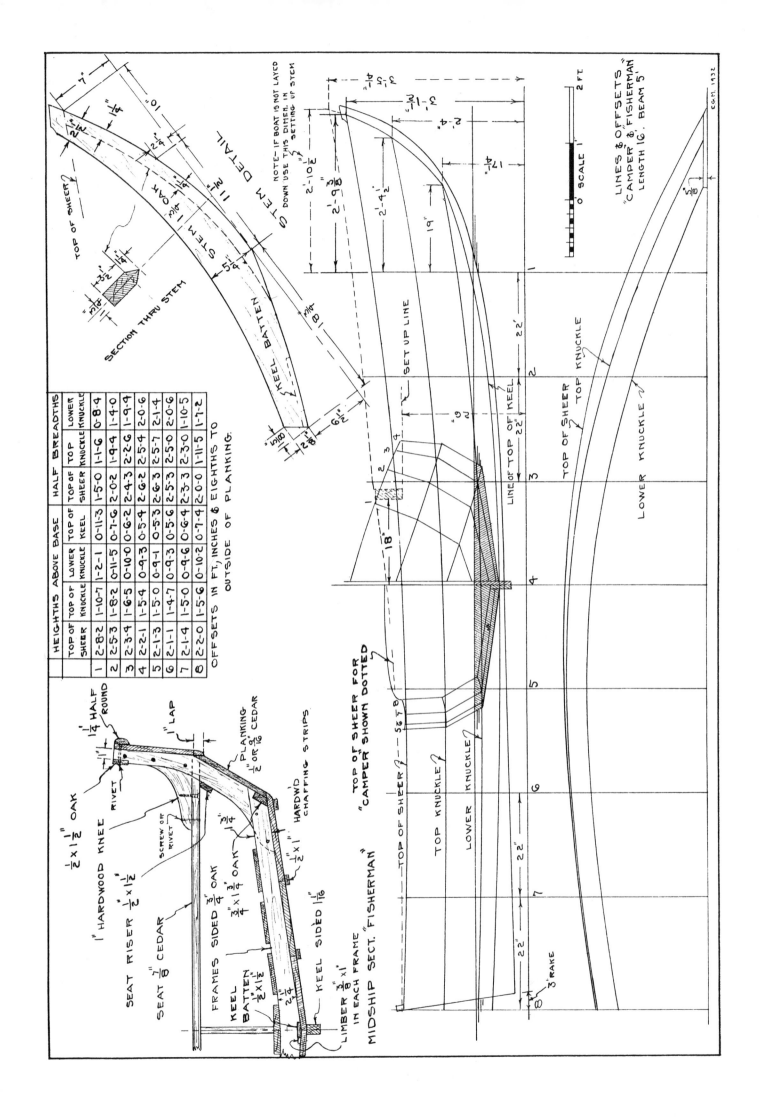

STEM DETAIL

SECTION THRU STEM

NOTE—IF BOAT IS NOT LAYED DOWN USE THIS DIMEN. IN SETTING UP STEM

KEEL BATTEN

STEM

OAK

TOP OF SHEER

	HEIGHTS ABOVE BASE				HALF BREADTHS		
	TOP OF SHEER	TOP OF KNUCKLE	LOWER KNUCKLE	TOP OF KEEL	TOP OF SHEER	TOP KNUCKLE	LOWER KNUCKLE
1	2-8-2	1-10-7	1-2-1	0-11-3	1-5-0	1-1-6	0-8-4
2	2-5-3	1-8-2	0-11-5	0-7-6	2-0-2	1-9-4	1-4-0
3	2-3-4	1-6-5	0-10-0	0-6-2	2-4-3	2-2-6	1-9-4
4	2-2-1	1-5-4	0-9-3	0-5-4	2-6-2	2-5-4	2-0-6
5	2-1-3	1-5-0	0-9-1	0-5-3	2-6-3	2-5-7	2-1-4
6	2-1-1	1-4-7	0-9-3	0-5-6	2-5-3	2-5-0	2-0-6
7	2-1-4	1-5-0	0-9-6	0-6-4	2-3-3	2-3-0	1-10-5
8	2-2-0	1-5-6	0-10-2	0-7-4	2-0-0	1-11-5	1-7-2

OFFSETS IN FT., INCHES & EIGHTHS TO OUTSIDE OF PLANKING.

SET UP LINE

LINE OF TOP OF KEEL

TOP OF SHEER

TOP KNUCKLE

LOWER KNUCKLE

"TOP OF SHEER FOR "CAMPER" SHOWN DOTTED

TOP OF SHEER

TOP KNUCKLE

LOWER KNUCKLE

MIDSHIP SECT. "FISHERMAN"

3° RAKE

SCALE 1"

O 1 2 FT.

LINES & OFFSETS "CAMPER & FISHERMAN" LENGTH 16', BEAM 5'

E.G.M. 1932

1" HARDWOOD KNEE

½" HALF ROUND OAK

1" LAP

PLANKING ½" OR ⅛" CEDAR

HARDWD CHAFFING STRIPS

SEAT RISER ½ × 1½

SEAT ⅞" CEDAR

SCREW OR RIVET

RIVET

FRAMES SIDED ¾" OAK
¾ × 1¼ OAK

½ × 1"

KEEL SIDED 1⅛

KEEL BATTEN ½ × 1½

LIMBER ⅜ × 1" IN EACH FRAME

Two Outboard Runabouts

THESE TWO OUTBOARD runabouts, one sixteen feet six inches long and the other fourteen feet eight inches, offer both a large and a small boat of a type lately become so popular. Both are of ample beam and freeboard, have a generous flare forward, and have the advantages of the front steering position with its better vision, all of which should make for safe, dry boats. A boat such as one of these is neither expensive nor hard to build, and being light is easily transported and handled. Its lightness also contributes not a little to a good turn of speed. It has many advantages over the heavier inboard powered runabout, and is ideal for summer home, lake, and inland water use.

The larger boat is intended for the higher-powered motors and has a reverse curve to fore and aft bottom lines designed to hold up the stern, making a level riding boat easily driven at high speeds. Speeds better than thirty miles may be expected with one of the higher-powered Class F motors.

The smaller boat is designed for lower powers and except for a slight curve in transom is of straight frame section, easily lofted and faired up. All short boats are prone to squat, but this one should give a good account of herself in similar company. About sixteen miles per hour may be expected with a 14 H. P. motor. It may be advisable to use steam or hot water on the forward ends of a few of the upper planks, but such thin plank should give little trouble.

Lumber Order for 16' 6" Runabout

Stem—1 pc. 1¾" × 10" N.—2' 6".
Forefoot—1 pc. 1¾" × 5" N .—4' 6".
Keel Batten—1 pc. ¾" × 1¾"—13'.
Frames—22' B. M. ⅝" thick, 6" wide and wider, 5' long and up.
Planking—Topsides—4 pcs. ⅜" × 6"—18', 4 pcs. ⅜" × 8"—18'.
Planking—Bottom—4 pcs. ⅜" × 8"—16', 4 pcs. ⅜" × 8"—18'.
Planking—Transom—3 pcs. ⅞" × 8"—4' 6" or 1 pc. 10"and 1 pc. 12".
Seam Battens—12 pcs. ⅜" × 1½"—18'.
Chines—2 pcs. 1¼" × 2" N.—18'.
Shelves—2 pcs. ¾" × 10"—13' and 1 pc. ¾" × 8"—8'.
Deck Beams—1 pc. ⅞" × 12"—10'.
Clamp—2 pcs. ½" × 1½"—8'.
Decking—50 B. M. ½" × 3" T. and G. and 2 pcs. ½" × 8"—12'.
Floor Boards—10 pcs. ½" × 3"—11' and 1 pc. ½" ×

6"—11' or 9 pcs. ½" × 4"—11'.
Seats—2 pcs. ¾" × 14"—5'.
Seats—Seat Backs—2 pcs. ½" × 18" plywood, 5' long, or 60 lineal ½" × 3" cedar.
Seats—Seat Braces—2 pcs. ¾" × 2½"—5'.
Cockpit Coaming—2 pcs. ½" × 4"—12' mahogany.
Cockpit Facer—1 pc. ½" × 6"—4' 6" mahogany.
Guards—2 pcs. 18' and 2 pcs. 6'—1" halfround.
Transom Knee—1 pc. 1" × 8"—2'.
Breasthook—1 pc. 2" × 6"—18" long, pine.

Lumber Order For 14' 8" Runabout

Stem—1 pc. 1¾" × 10"—2' 6".
Forefoot—1 pc. 1¾" × 5"—4'.
Keel Batten—1 pc. ¾" × 1¾"—12'.
Frames—20 B. M. ⅝" thick, 6" wide or wider, 5' long and up.
Planking—Topsides—6 pcs. ⅜" × 6"—16' and 2 pcs. ⅜" × 8"—16'.
Planking—Bottom—8 pcs. ⅜" × 8"—16'.
Planking—Transom—2 pcs. ⅞" × 10"—4'.
Seam Battens—12 pcs. ⅜" × 1½"—16'.
Chines—2 pcs. 1¼" × 2" N.—16'.
Shelves—2 pcs. ¾" × 8"—12' and 1 pc. ¾" × 8"—8'.
Beams—1 pc. ⅞" × 12"—9'.
Clamp—2 pcs. ½" × 1½"—8'.
Decking—50 B. M. ½" × 3" T. and G. and 2 pcs. ½" × 8"—11'.
Floor Boards—10 pcs. ½" × 3"—10' and 1 pc. ½" × 6"—10', or 8 pcs. ½" × 4"—10'.
Cockpit Coaming—2 pcs. ½" × 4"—10'.
Cockpit Facer—1 pc. ½" × 6"—4'.
Guards—2 pcs. 16' and 2 pcs. 6'—1" halfround.

Seats, transom knee and breasthook same as 16' boat.

These two runabouts are so similar that the construction plans of the larger boat will do for both, and in the following they will be treated as one.

The construction methods and details in the text of this book will apply closely here, and the following is intended to fill in the gaps and treat this craft individually.

The stem and forefoot are shown in separate detail, and these and the body plan only need be laid down, but as explained elsewhere considerable may be gained by completely lofting the boat. The boat is erected bottom side up as in Fig. No. 9, and as the sheerline is straight we will take advantage of this in setting up the boat by placing on it the bottom edge of the cross-bands, as in Fig. No. 5. The erecting stringers must be set up with after ends higher than forward, in order to place the boat on an even keel. In the sixteen-foot boat the aft end should be 5" higher, and in the fourteen-foot boat 4¾" (note dotted line above lines of the latter boat). The stringers should be about thirty-six inches apart.

The frames are assembled exactly as in Fig. No. 5; the transom is set up first and fastened in place much as in Fig. No. 9. Set it and all the frames plumb, which in this case is not square off the stringers (up and down) on account of their slant. Stem and forefoot are fastened together on the bench and let into frames Nos. 1 and 2, so that the bearding line is flush with edge of frames, as in the small detail inserted in inboard profile. When assembling frames No. 1 and No. 2 a slot 1¾" wide should be provided and the frame floor so placed that with a little fitting the forefoot will fit snugly in place.

The keel batten is scarfed into forefoot, as shown, and tapers from here to ½" × 1¾" at frame No. 5 and aft. Fasten to each frame with two 1½" No. 8 screws. There is an inner chine only and its layout is explained in text matter. Little steaming should be necessary with such thin plank. The bottom is planked first and trims off flush with outside of chine from frame No. 2 aft, but forward the edge rolls up until it is almost square at stem, as shown in details inserted in lines drawings of sixteen-foot boat; in the smaller boat go back to station No. 3. Trim a spot at stem and another at about station No. 1, also trim plank edge flush from station No. 3 aft and tack a light batten along edge to stem and trim to this with a chisel and rabbet plane. Put glue between plank and chine and fasten to chine with 1" No. 8 screws or copper boat nails clinched inside. The side planks are next, but cannot be finished until the shelf is in. The two lower strakes on each side (next to chine) however, should be put on and if possible the third.

The boat may now be turned over and well braced in the new position. The cross-bands will have to be dropped six or eight inches to clear the shelf and clamp, in each case fasten the new cross-band before removing the old one, and from amidship aft alternate ones may be omitted. The sheerline is faired up and the clamp and deck beams installed, as described under "Beams, Shelf and Clamp." The clamp extends aft from stem to the last deck beam only.

The shelf, as shown, is 4½" wide, tapering to about 2" at stem, and is notched over frames aft of deck only, and here it is fastened through each frame with a 16d galvanized nail, counterbored for head and set in flush with frame. Fasten beams to shelf as shown in detail. The 1" oak transom knees are screw-fastened from aft side of transom, also through the shelf into the hardwood knee. The side planking may now be completed.

The two ½" × 8" pieces ordered for decking are intended for covering boards each side of cockpit, and should be allowed to extend forward over deck beams, and the forward decking fitted against them. If deck is canvased the latter should turn down over the last beam and is covered by the cockpit facer, and where it crosses the covering boards it is tucked under and fastened across face of covering board by a row of tacks.

If a varnished or bright deck is decided upon, the covering board should run to stem about as shown by dotted line. In this case the shelf should be wide enough to take deck ends, or else fillers fastened to it, furring it out sufficiently. For this purpose see "The Deck."

The windshield frame should be made at a cabinet shop. Provide the shop man with a pattern fitted to deck crown at the right angle and cut to length. A slatted seat back is shown in midsection and a solid one in the small plan; the latter is of plywood and the builder may use either. I am sure there is little need of further explanation and the balance of the job will be left to you.

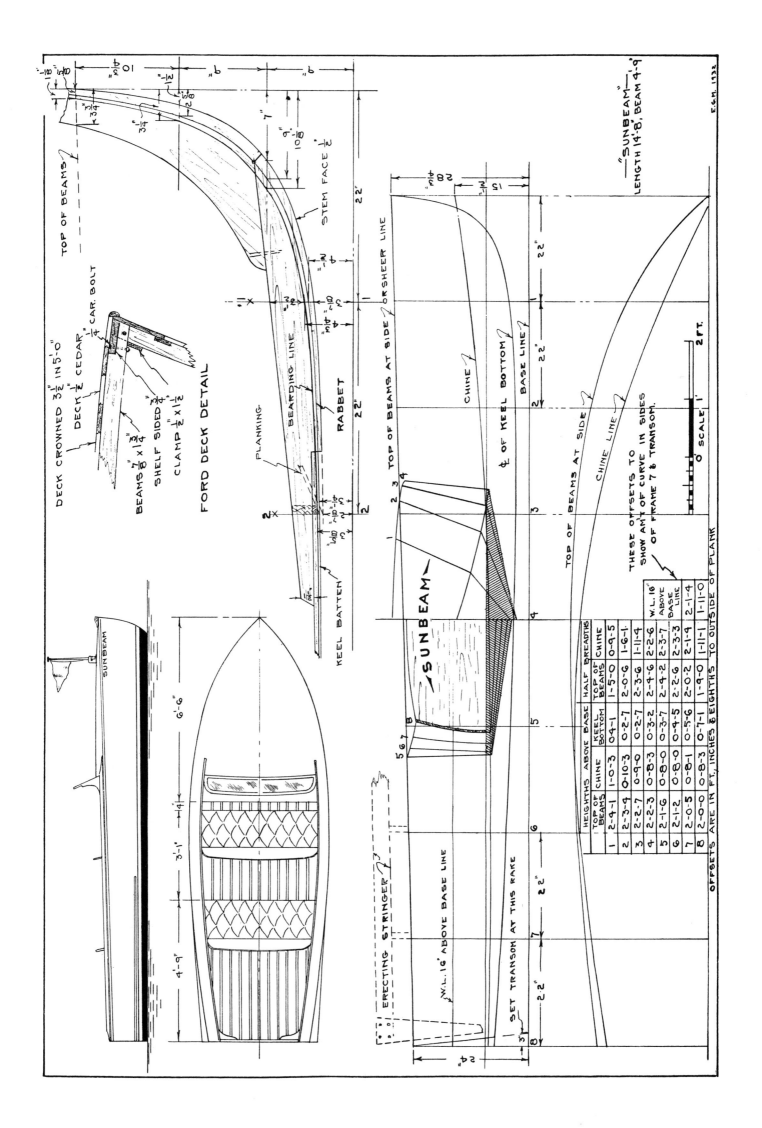

"SUNBEAM"
LENGTH 14'-8", BEAM 4'-9"

E.&M. 1132

FORD DECK DETAIL

DECK CROWNED 3½" IN 5'-0"

TOP OF BEAMS

DECK ½" CEDAR
¼" CAR. BOLT
BEAMS ⅞" × 1¾"
SHELF SIDED ¾"
CLAMP ½ × 1½

PLANKING
BEARING LINE
STEM FACE ½"
RABBET
KEEL BATTEN

TOP OF BEAMS AT SIDE OR SHEER LINE
CHINE
℄ OF KEEL BOTTOM
BASE LINE

TOP OF BEAMS AT SIDE
CHINE LINE

THESE OFFSETS TO
SHOW AM'T OF CURVE IN SIDES
OF FRAME 7 & TRANSOM.

SUNBEAM

SUNBEAM

ERECTING STRINGER
W.L. 16' ABOVE BASE LINE
SET TRANSOM AT THIS RAKE

0 SCALE 1'   2 FT.

HEIGHTS ABOVE BASE			HALF BREADTHS		
	TOP OF BEAMS	CHINE	KEEL BOTTOM	TOP OF BEAMS	CHINE
1	2-4-1	1-0-3	0-4-1	1-5-0	0-9-5
2	2-3-4	0-10-3	0-2-7	2-0-6	1-6-1
3	2-2-7	0-9-0	0-2-7	2-3-6	1-11-4
4	2-2-3	0-8-3	0-3-2	2-4-6	2-2-6
5	2-1-6	0-8-0	0-3-7	2-4-2	2-3-7
6	2-1-2	0-8-0	0-4-5	2-2-6	2-3-3
7	2-0-5	0-8-1	0-5-6	2-0-2	2-1-4
8	2-0-0	0-8-3	0-7-1	1-9-0	1-11-1	1-11-0

W.L. 16"
ABOVE
BASE
LINE

OFFSETS ARE IN FT., INCHES & EIGHTHS TO OUTSIDE OF PLANK

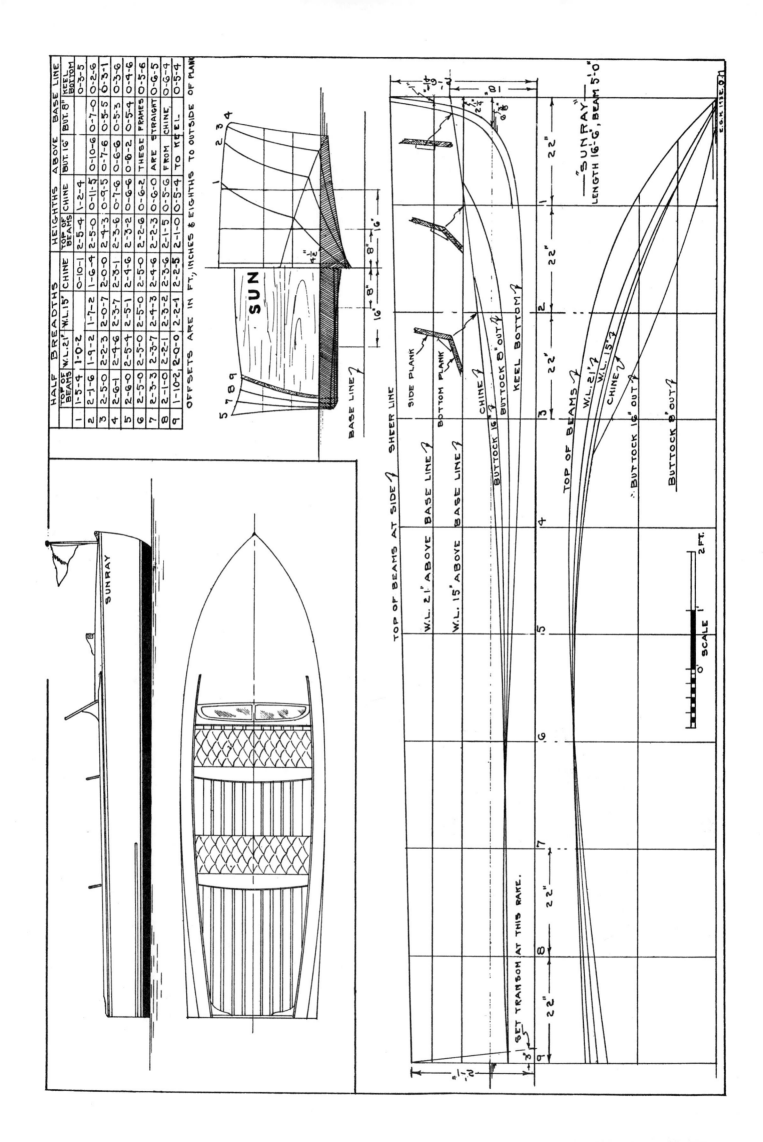

"SUNRAY" LENGTH 16'-6", BEAM 5'-0"

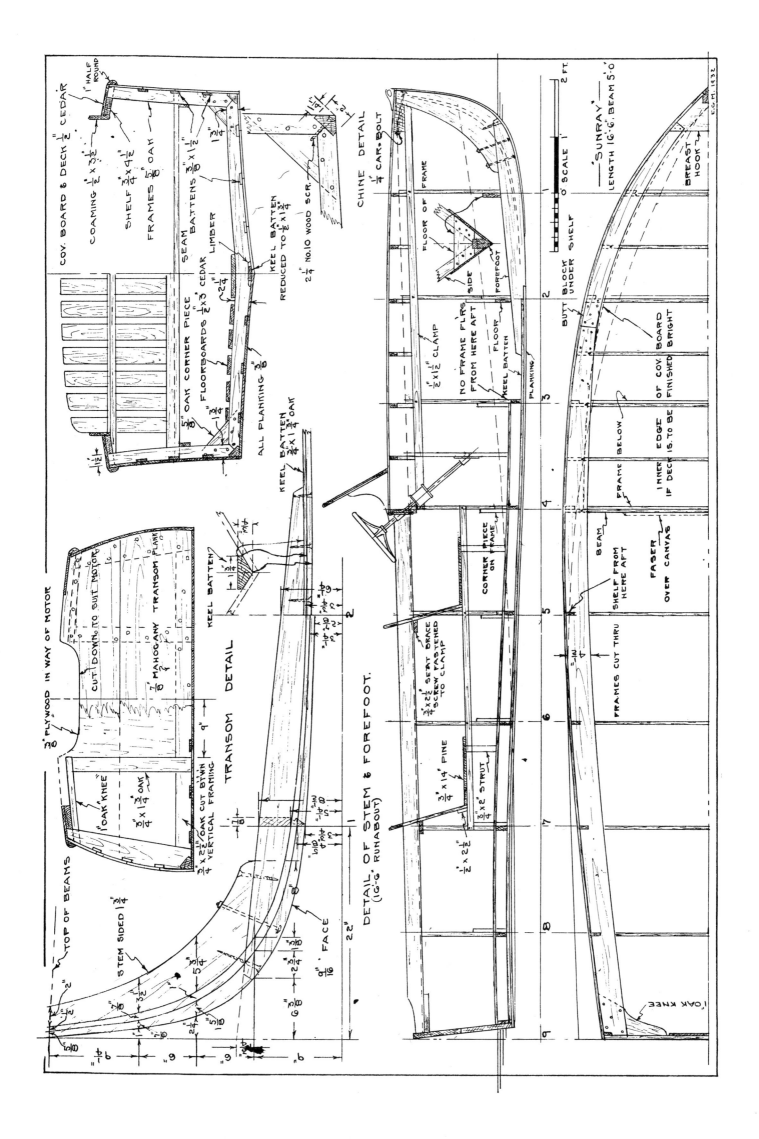

"SUNRAY"
LENGTH 16'·6". BEAM 5'·0

E.G.M. 1932

CHINE DETAIL

COV. BOARD & DECK ½" CEDAR
COAMING ½" x 3½"
SHELF ¾" x 4½"
FRAMES ⅝" OAK
SEAM BATTENS ⅜" x 1½"
LIMBER
⅝" OAK CORNER PIECE
FLOORBOARDS 2 x 3" CEDAR
KEEL BATTEN REDUCED TO ½" x 1¾"
2¼" No.10 WOOD SCR.
ALL PLANKING ⅜"

½" PLYWOOD IN WAY OF MOTOR
CUT DOWN TO SUIT MOTOR
⅞" MAHOGANY TRANSOM PLANK
KEEL BATTEN
1" OAK KNEE
⅝" x 1¾" OAK
¾" x 2½" OAK CUT B'TW'N VERTICAL FRAMING

TRANSOM DETAIL

TOP OF BEAMS
STEM SIDED 1¾"
9" FACE

DETAIL OF STEM & FOREFOOT.
(16'·6" RUNABOUT)

½" x 1½" CLAMP
FLOOR OF FRAME
SIDE
FOREFOOT
FLOOR
KEEL BATTEN
PLANKING
NO FRAME FLRS FROM HERE AFT
CORNER PIECE ON FRAME
¾" x 2½" SEAT BRACE ¼ SCREW FASTENED TO CLAMP
¾" x 1¼" PINE
⅝" x 2" STRUT
½" x 2½"

BUTT BLOCK UNDER SHELF
BREAST HOOK ?
FRAME BELOW
INNER EDGE OF COV. BOARD IF DECK IS TO BE FINISHED BRIGHT
BEAM
FASER OVER CANVAS
SHELF FROM HERE AFT
FRAMES CUT THRU
1" OAK KNEE

"Mariner,"
An Outboard Cruiser

THIS BOAT IS a miniature of the boat illustrated, a larger cruiser designed by the author, a good sea boat of trim appearance that met with favorable comment. It is intended as a complete little cruiser for two or three, and contains a large cockpit, berths, galley, and toilet, which, after all, is the nucleus of any yacht. In the small cruiser it is difficult to turn out a nice-appearing hull and still have workable headroom. In this case the large hatch in the galley provides for this where it is most needed, and there is four feet six inches headroom under the trunk beams. Forward there is a man-sized hatch, and the boat may be made fast or anchor handled without climbing on deck. A folding card table will serve as a dining-table in the cockpit, and folding camp-stools are suggested; also a canvas cot will accommodate an extra voyager.

The Lumber Order

Keel—1 pc. 2½" × 11½"—18'.
Stem—1 pc. 2½" × 7"—4' 6".
Knee—2½" natural crook or 1 pc. 2½" × 12"—3'.
Framing—50 B. M. ¾" oak, 4' long and up.
Seam Battens—20 pcs. ⅜" × 1¾"—20'.
Side Plank—12 pcs. ½" × 6"—20', 2 pcs. ½" × 8"—20'.
Bottom Plank—8 pcs. ½" × 8"—20' and 4 pcs. ½" × 6"—18' (includes transom).
Keel Batten—1 pc. ⅞" × 4½"—15'.
Chine—2 pcs. ¾" × 2½"—20' and 2 pcs. ¾" × 1⅝"—20'.
Clamp—2 pcs. ¾" × 12"—8' (Cockpit).
Decking—100 B. M. ½" × 3" ceiling, V joint one side.
Beams—3 pcs. ⅞" × 12"—6'.
Cockpit and Cabin Floor—100' ¾" ceiling.
Shelf—4 pcs. 1¹⁄₁₆" × 10"—8'.
Trunk—2 pcs. ⅞" × 10"—8' and 1 pc. ⅞" × 10"—5'.
Bulkheads—2 pcs. 24" × 60" main, 1 pc. 30" × 42" chain L. and 2 pcs. 24" × 36" galley, all ½" plywood (waterproof).
Covering Board—1 pc. ⅝" × 12"—8' and 1 pc. ⅝" × 6"—6'.
For'd Chocks—1 pc. 2½" × 10"—5'.
Posts for Tops—2 pcs. 1¼" × 1¼"—5' 6".
Top—2 pcs. ¾" × 1¾"—9' sides, 1 pc. ¾" × 8"—6' 6" ends, beams—1 pc. ¾" × 10"—6' 6", battens—6 pcs. ⅜" × 1¾"—9'.
Guards—2 pcs. 1" × 2"—17', 1 pc. ¾" × 1¼"—14'—aft, and 2 pcs. ¾" × 1¼"—12'—for'd deck.
Trim—36 Lin. Ft. ½" × 1¾" and 1 pc. ½" × 12"—6' 6" mahogany (trunk and top).

In addition you will need about one hundred feet of cedar or pine ½" or ¾" thick for interior finish, berths, drawers, lockers, etc., but as there will be various odds and ends of planking on hand it would perhaps be best to order this item later. A steam box will be required for the garboard and adjacent planking; also some of the top planking.

The construction methods and details in the text of this book will apply closely here, and the following is intended to fill in the gaps and treat this craft individually.

This boat will have to be completely lofted, as the stations represent every other frame, and the intermediate frames must be struck in after the lines are all faired up. These are first drawn in on the half-breadth and profile and then picked up with a batten and transferred to the body plan, much as the faired-up lines are checked back to body plan, as explained under "Lofting." Top of guard must be marked on the frames, as it is also the top of the first side plank. Put cross-bands on alternate frames only, and keep them about six inches above top of guard line to clear shelf later. The frame is assembled as in Fig. No. 5. See "Installing the Outboard Motor," for depth of transom.

The boat is erected as in Fig. No. 10 and the keel batten is best bevelled before fastening it to the keel, although this can be done later with a rabbet plane. Fasten to keel with 16d galvanized nails. If the natural crook forefoot knee is substituted by a straight-grain piece it should be straighter inside to avoid too much cross-grain.

The frames with cross-bands are set up first, plumbed, braced, etc., and the others slipped in after boat is all set up and bottom ribband is in place. The chine is next, and use two 1¾" No. 10 screws through inner chine into frame and 1¼" No. 8 screws to fasten outer chine to inner. The shelf is put in now and the forward piece is placed 1 1/16" below sheerline or top of beams and the aft piece is placed with top to sheerline and laps over forward piece as shown. Scale after shelf widths from plan, fasten into shelf through frames, using 3" No. 12 screws, check camber or tilt of shelf before fastening, using a deck beam.

It is much easier to put in the ½" plywood bulkhead on frame No. 3½ before planking, and the forward deck beams also. The bulkhead must extend high enough to take trunk beam later, and at the side it cuts off flush with top of shelf, and plumb up from its inside edge. Tack a batten to frames each side of cockpit to represent top of planking, and cut frames off to this line and to beam camber, so covering board will have same camber as deck.

As previously stated, place top edge of first plank at the guard mark from station No. 2 aft, but let it run up, where it will, from here forward. Fillers must be fitted between frames on top of forward shelf to receive plank and guard fastenings. Steaming will be necessary in this job, especially at garboard and sheer forward. Fasten plank to frames with 1¼" galvanized boat nails, and to seam battens with 1" copper boat nails clinched inside.

With sheer strake trimmed flush with top of beams, we are ready for the deck, which should be fastened with 4d galvanized wire nails. The cockpit clamps are next and then the covering board or rail; this butts against decking and fastens with 1½" No. 10 screws, into fillers, plank edge and clamp. Use a batten to obtain correct length of clamp.

Before canvasing for'd deck, plane a flat spot at edges for guards, as explained under that item. The deck may now be canvased, and cut canvas an inch or so long to be turned up inside of trunk later and covered by the facer. The trunk rests on top of the canvas, as shown, fitting the for'd piece first, making it 6¾" above deck at ends, as dimensioned on lines drawing. Trim ends plumb and fit trunk sides against them and the bulkhead aft. I would put sides in place and scribe the bottom to fit deck, then on the bench cut out the three little windows. These must be rabbeted for glass, which is best done on a shaper at a cabinet shop. First bore each corner with an expansion bit and saw out between and trim up the edges. The shaper guide will travel around this edge and neatly rabbet it. The windows may have square corners if you wish, in which case they are more easily rabbeted by hand than if round. Between the bolt fastenings shown use 2½" No. 12 screws through shelf into trunk. Taper for'd end of trunk to about 1½" and through-fasten to shelf and filler with two ¼" carriage bolts, one set up under shelf and one under filler. The bolt heads should be ground down to fit a ½" plug hole. The outboard profile shows aft end of trunk finished with a slight ogee; this is optional and if done the shelf and decking must extend beyond bulkhead to take care of this.

Trunk beams cut through trunk at each end of beam. The cockpit floor may be canvased or covered with linoleum. If you ceil the sides here use ⅜" tongue and groove, and bore some vent holes through clamp between frames to eliminate dead air and the resultant dry rot. The toilet should have the regulation seacocks, and it is a good plan to keep the discharge above waterline, but still in the green paint.

A light composition panel may be laid on canopy beams instead of the battens, in which case do not droop the for'd end as shown, but hold same crown everywhere. Insulate around stove with ¼" asbestos* and light galvanized iron. The interior finish and balance of the job should offer no difficulty.

---

*Asbestos is extremely hazardous—use a substitute if possible.

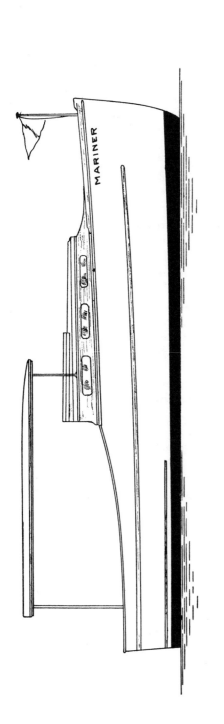

MARINER

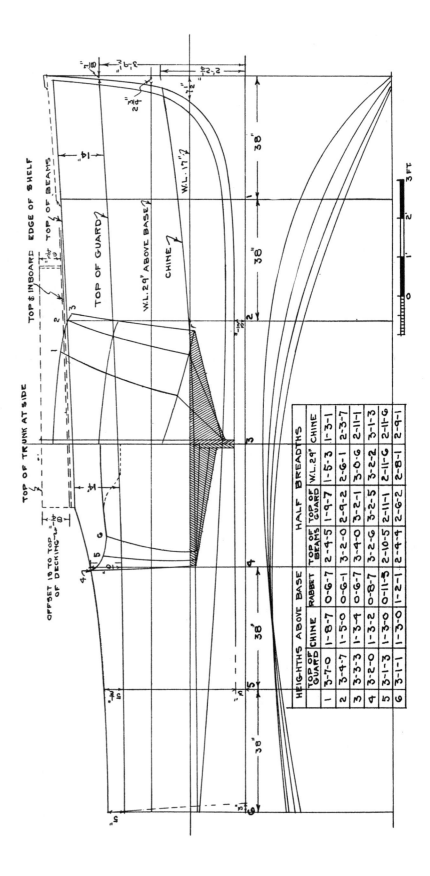

TOP & INBOARD EDGE OF SHELF

TOP OF BEAMS

TOP OF GUARD

W.L. 29" ABOVE BASE

CHINE

W.L. 17"½

TOP OF TRUNK AT SIDE

OFFSET 1⅛ TO TOP OF DECKING

3 FT

	HEIGHTS ABOVE BASE			HALF BREADTHS		
	TOP OF GUARD	CHINE	RABBET	TOP OF BEAMS	TOP OF GUARD	W.L. 29"	CHINE
1	3-7-0	1-8-7	0-6-7	2-4-5	1-9-7	1-5-3	1-3-1
2	3-4-7	1-5-0	0-6-1	3-2-0	2-9-2	2-6-1	2-3-7
3	3-3-3	1-3-4	0-6-7	3-4-0	3-2-1	3-0-6	2-11-1
4	3-2-0	1-3-2	0-8-7	3-2-6	3-2-5	3-2-2	3-1-3
5	3-1-3	1-3-0	0-11-5	2-10-5	2-11-1	2-11-6	2-11-6
6	3-1-1	1-3-0	1-2-1	2-4-4	2-6-2	2-8-1	2-9-1

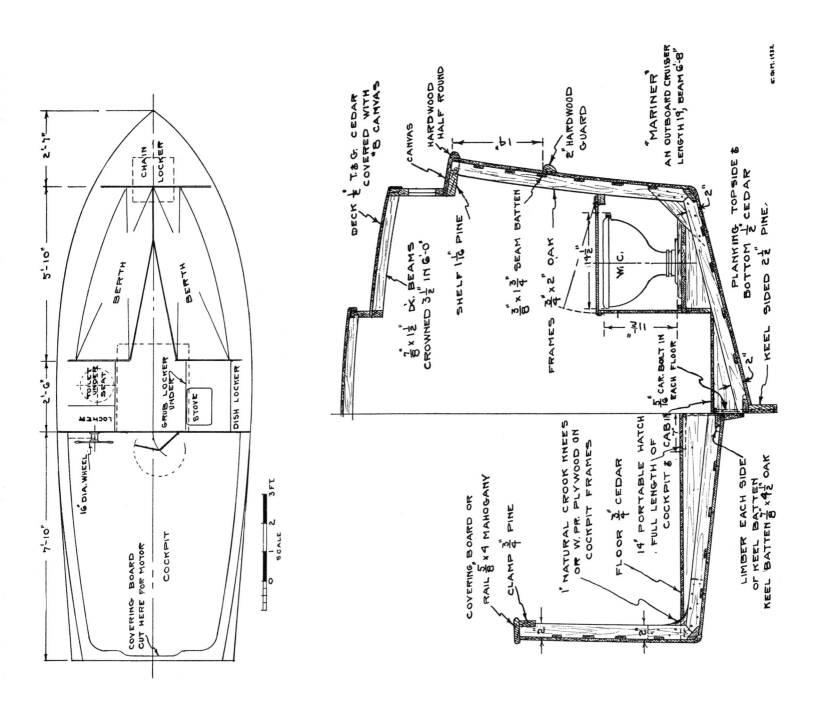

COVERING BOARD
CUT HERE FOR MOTOR

7'-10"

5'-10"

2'-7"

2'-6"

CHAIN LOCKER

BERTH

BERTH

COCKPIT

16" DIA. WHEEL

⅜ CHAIN LOCKER

TOILET UNDER SEAT

GRUB LOCKER UNDER

STOVE

DISH LOCKER

SCALE
0   1   2   3 FT

DECK ⅞" T.&.G. CEDAR
COVERED WITH
#8 CANVAS

CANVAS

HARDWOOD HALF ROUND

2" HARDWOOD GUARD

"6"

⅞" x 1½" DK. BEAMS
CROWNED 3½" IN 6'-0"

SHELF 1⅛" PINE

⅜" x 1¾" SEAM BATTEN

FRAMES ¾" x 2" OAK

1½"

11 ½"

2"

W.C.

2"

⁵⁄₁₆" CAR. BOLT IN
EACH FLOOR

COVERING BOARD OR
RAIL ⅝" x 4" MAHOGANY

CLAMP ¾" PINE

1" NATURAL CROOK KNEES
OR W.PR. PLYWOOD ON
COCKPIT FRAMES

FLOOR ¾" CEDAR

14' PORTABLE HATCH
FULL LENGTH OF
COCKPIT & CABIN

2"

2"

LIMBER EACH SIDE
OF KEEL BATTEN
KEEL BATTEN ⅞" x 4½" OAK

KEEL SIDED 2½"

PLANKING, TOPSIDE &
BOTTOM ½" CEDAR

"MARINER"
AN OUTBOARD CRUISER
LENGTH 19', BEAM 6'-8"

C.G.M. 1932

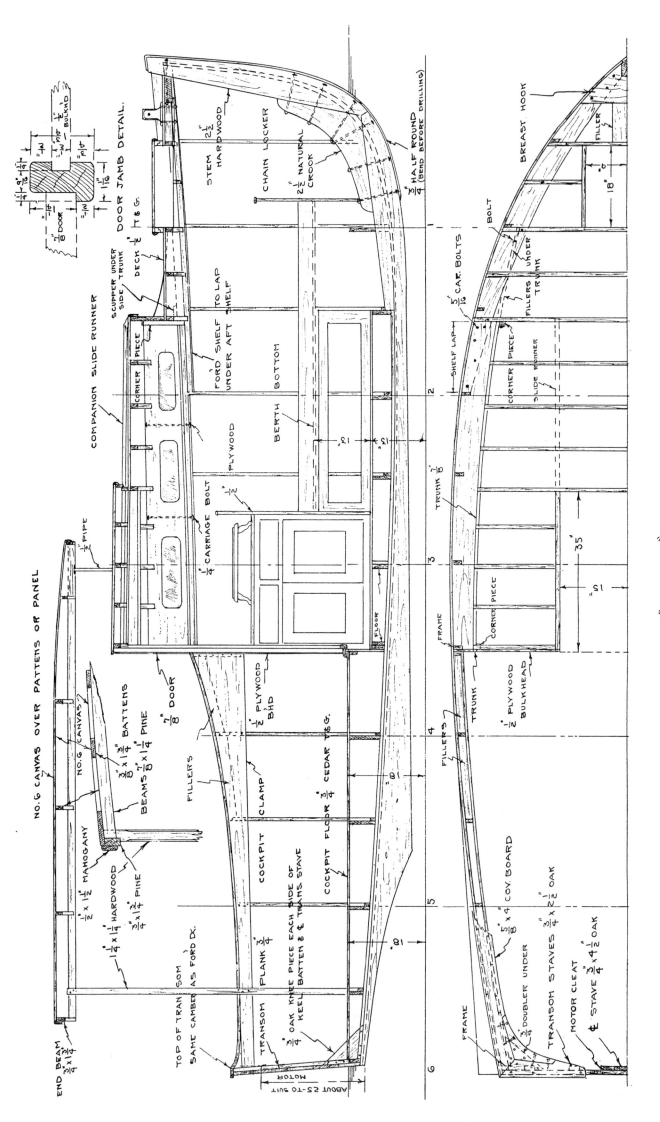

— "MARINER" —
AN OUTBOARD CRUISER
LENGTH 19', BEAM 6'-8"

0   SCALE 1'   2 FT.   C.G.M. 1132

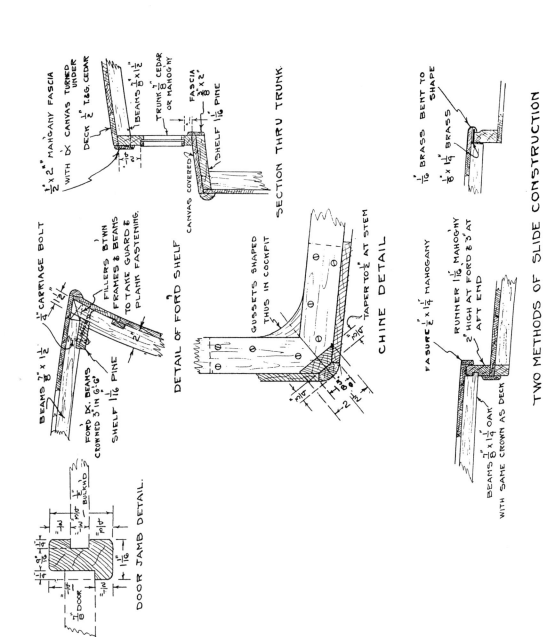

$\frac{1}{2}"\times 2\frac{1}{4}"$ MAHGANY FASCIA
WITH DK CANVAS TURNED UNDER
DECK $\frac{1}{2}"$ T.&G. CEDAR

BEAMS $\frac{7}{8}"\times 1\frac{1}{2}"$

TRUNK $\frac{7}{8}"$ CEDAR OR MAHOGNY

FASCIA $\frac{3}{8}"\times 2"$

SHELF $1\frac{1}{16}$ PINE

CANVAS COVERED

SECTION THRU TRUNK.

$\frac{1}{4}"$ CARRIAGE BOLT

FILLERS BTWN FRAMES & BEAMS TO TAKE GUARD & PLANK FASTENING.

BEAMS $\frac{7}{8}"\times 1\frac{1}{2}"$

FORD DK. BEAMS CROWNED 3" IN 6' 6"

SHELF $1\frac{1}{16}$ PINE

DETAIL OF FORD SHELF

GUSSETS SHAPED THUS IN COCKPIT

TAPER TO $2\frac{1}{2}"$ AT STEM

CHINE DETAIL.

$\frac{1}{16}"$ BRASS BENT TO SHAPE

$\frac{1}{8}"\times 1\frac{1}{4}"$ BRASS

FASURE $\frac{1}{2}"\times 1\frac{1}{4}"$ MAHOGANY

RUNNER $1\frac{1}{16}$ MAHOGNY 2" HIGH AT FORD & 3" AT AFT END

BEAMS $\frac{7}{8}"\times 1\frac{1}{4}"$ OAK WITH SAME CROWN AS DECK

TWO METHODS OF SLIDE CONSTRUCTION

DOOR JAMB DETAIL.

BULKHD

$\frac{7}{8}"$ DOOR

—"MARINER"—
AN OUTBOARD CRUISER

"Wasp,"
An Outboard Racer

THE SPORT OF outboard racing has in late years advanced by leaps and bounds, and it is not hard to recall when ten and twelve miles per hour were records to shoot at. Improvement in hull and motor design and, of course, much higher horsepowers are responsible for speeds that not so long ago would have been considered impossible. The author designed and built one of the first outboard step boats, and it gave a very good account of itself, but the advantages of this type of hull could not be fully demonstrated with the heavy and low-powered motors then available.

The design is modelled after several very successful boats and differs in no radical respect from them. The beam is generous, but the actual planing surface and width has been kept within recognized standards. Similar boats have been very successful in classes B to E. Lighter scantlings are specified for the lower-powered motors, and the boat is large enough to carry the E. and F. power plants.

The slight round at outer edge of bottom is a modification of the "anti trips" on the *Humarock Baby*, and similar but more pronounced than on Don Flower's *Falcon*, both top-notch boats.

The National Outboard Association* stipulates that the useful and necessary weight of hull, with steering-wheel and motor controls, shall not be less than the following:

Class A—100 pounds, Class B—150 pounds, Class C—190 pounds; not to include cushions, temporary seats, fire extinguishers, gas tanks, and life preservers. No ballast is allowable and all weights shall be useful and necessary. This is the major stipulation, but there are other minor ones.

As the rules are revised from time to time, you had best consult the latest rule book, which should be available at your local yacht or outboard club.

The Lumber Order

Keel—2 pcs. ¾″ × 2″—7′ spruce.
Frames—15 B. M. ⅝″ × 6″ (and wider) spruce, 5′ long and up.
Web Frames—2 pcs. ¼″ × 18″—48″ plywood.
Deck Battens—2 pcs. ½″ × 1″—12′.
Chine—2 pcs. ½″ × 1½″—7′ and 2 pcs. ½″ × 4″—7′ spruce.
Seam Battens—6 pcs. ⅜″ × 1½″—12′ spruce.
Side Plank—2 pcs. ⅜″ × 11″—12′.

---

*No longer in operation.

Bottom Plank—8 pcs. ⁵⁄₁₆″ × 8″—6′—aft; 6 pcs. ⁵⁄₁₆″ × 8″—7′ and 2 pcs. ⁵⁄₁₆″ × 8″—5′—for'd.
Transom—1 pc. 1″ × 14″—5′.
Deck Beams—1 pc. ½″ × 12″—5′; header, 1 pc. ½″ × 5½″—6′.
Deck Stringers—2 pcs. ¼″ × 8″—9′ spruce.
Cockpit Corner Piece—1 pc. 2″ × 8″–2′ 6″ cedar or spruce.
Guards—2 pcs. ¾″ halfround—12′.
Headlog—1 pc. 3″ × 4″—9″ long, pine or fir.
Transom Knee—1″ natural crook or 1 pc. 1″ × 8″—18″ oak.

Plank scraps will make cockpit coaming and frame scraps the stub beams. No steaming is required in the construction of this boat.

The construction methods and details in the text of this book will apply closely here, and the following is intended to fill in the gaps and treat this craft individually.

This boat is first lofted as in the usual manner to the projected knuckle or chine lines, indicated by the dotted lines. The curved edges of bottom are then marked on each station by use of a curve or radius pattern, which is made of cardboard or thin board, as per small sketch. Scribe the twenty-four-inch radius as shown and the other dimensions will be found about correct. Slide the pattern out on each frame station until the dimension D is as marked on sheer plan. Station No. 6, for example, will be curved up from the straight line ⅝″, as shown. The plank thickness is then marked off all stations and frames themselves cut to this shape.

The ¼″ plywood webs are placed between side and bottom pieces of frame and the whole well glued and screw-fastened, using ¾″ No. 6 screws and larger in laps. Beams on frames Nos. 2 and 4 must be laid out to specified camber and fastened to the frames. On frame No. 6 allow the web frame to project above the sheerline enough to fasten the short beams to later. The cross-bands are fastened to frames Nos. 1, 2, 4, and 6 only, and with bottom edges on sheerline as in Fig. No. 5. They should be at least 3½″ wide and it may be necessary to cut out a half inch or so from top of stringer for the beam on frame No. 4, and make cross-band on frame No. 1 three feet long. In the body plan of lines drawing the for'd face of the headlog is dimensioned; the plank thickness must be deducted from sides and bottom and by taking the bevels from the plan and headlog may be gotten out. The transom should have the ⅝″ × 1½″ frame pieces fastened to its outer edge, as shown.

The boat is erected upside down, as in Fig. No. 9. Place erecting stringers thirty-two inches apart inside to inside and place them level fore and aft; the slight sheer will be disregarded. Frames Nos. 1, 2, 4, and 6 and the transom are now set up, and transom must rake 1¾″, as shown.

The two deck battens are next and the headlog is fastened between them, as shown. Before fastening the latter, check length required for side plank as it will be nip and tuck, and you may find it necessary to move headlog aft a trifle. The for'd chine batten should be sawed to fit the curve without edge bending. In fitting the aft chine place a piece of the bottom planking between it and step frame in order that the space between the two will be the exact plank thickness. In the section marked "just aft of step" the arrow and the X will show what is meant. Fasten deck battens and chine battens to frames with 1½" No. 8 screws.

The intermediate frames may now be fitted, also the ½" × 2" intermediate floors forward; these will stiffen the bottom where the greatest punishment occurs. The for'd keel batten may be tapered to ⅜" at headlog and the aft piece will extend to frame No. 3, and when the garboard planks aft of step are in place the two keel battens are bolted together, as per detail. The oak knee at centre of transom should be installed now, and use 1¾" No. 10 screws through transom and keel batten. Fasten keel battens to frames with 1¾" No. 10 screws. The seam battens are fastened with 1" No. 8 screws, but do not fasten aft battens or aft keel batten to topside of frame No. 4 yet.

The bottom aft of step is planked first, glue well to battens, etc., and use 1" No. 6 brass screws in frames, transom, keel, and chine battens. Fasten to the step frame or No. 4 from inside, also fastening each seam batten here as it is reached by the planking. In the battens use ¾" copper boat nails clinched inside, as explained under "The Dory Lap." As a smooth bottom is really important it is best to hand plane the bottom plank before putting them on. Later a large file may be used to smooth up the nail heads and the whole sanded smooth. After the for'd bottom plank are on, trim the edges flush with chine battens and put on the side plank; use ¾" No. 6 screws in chine battens.

Turn the boat over now and put in the balance of the deck beams and the headers. The latter will not be straight on top, so spring a batten on top of beams Nos. 2, 3, and 4 to transom and obtain the correct shape, also obtain crown of beam at frame No. 3 in same manner. The transom, sheer strake, and deck header are trimmed off three-eighths inch for the plywood knees, which should be glued and screw-fastened using 1" No. 6 wood screws. The deck stringers should be glued to the knees and elsewhere and screw-fastened to beams, etc.; use ¾" copper boat nails clinched in the transom knees. The cockpit corner piece for'd will have to be shaped from the thick piece ordered so that top edge will conform with crown of beams; hold outer edge flush with top of deck stringers.

The deck is covered with No. 10 duck turned down around edges and covered by the ¾" halfround guard on the outside and by the ³⁄₁₆" × 1½" coaming inside as shown. The inside edge of deck stringer will form a ledge ¼" high and beams may be shimmed up to it with a wedge-shaped shim, as shown in step section; also the sheer strake for'd of stringer must be shimmed. The stem face piece is shaped roughly and trimmed up after fastening; the halfround guard around it must be sawed to shape from a piece of ¾" stock.

Finish sides of hull bright or paint, just as you wish, but I would in either case paint the bottom; flushing all dents, screw heads, etc., with smoothing compound and sand between each coat, to obtain as smooth a finish as possible; finish with pumice stone and sweet oil. The fin may be purchased and is best through-bolted to keel batten. After steering gear and motor controls are installed the boat should be weighed. You still have a little leeway in the weight of floor boards to bring the boat up to the weight minimum; also the rule book suggests, "If you must increase the weight of hull, use strengthening braces."

If building for Class B and C, change bottom plank to ¼", web frames to ³⁄₁₆", keel to ½" × 2", and omit the ⅞" oak transom knee.

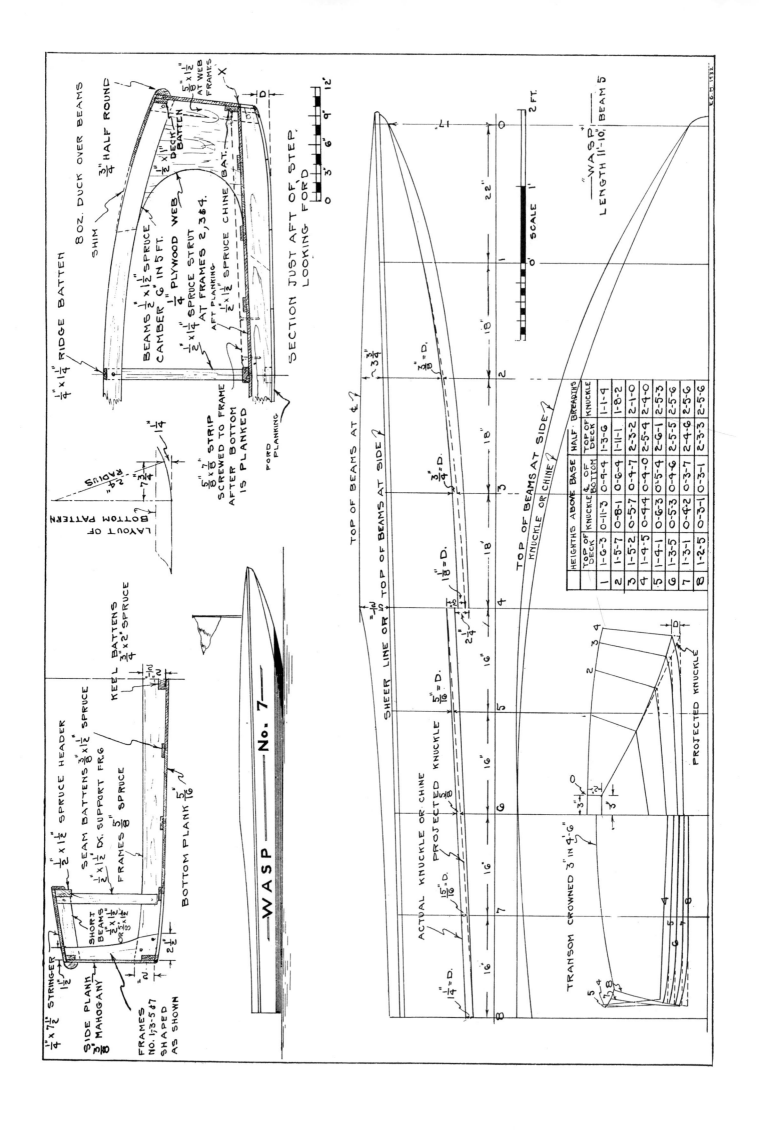

SECTION JUST AFT OF STEP.
LOOKING FORD

8 OZ. DUCK OVER BEAMS
¾" HALF ROUND
SHIM
¼"×1¼" RIDGE BATTEN
5/8"×1½" AT WEB FRAMES
DECK BATTEN
X
BEAMS ½"×1½" SPRUCE CAMBER 6" IN 5 FT.
¼" PLYWOOD WEB
2"×1¼" SPRUCE STRUT AT FRAMES 2, 3&4.
½"×1½" SPRUCE CHINE BAT.
AFT PLANKING
D
FORD PLANKING

LAYOUT OF BOTTOM PATTERN
2¼" RADIUS
7¾"
¼"
5/8"×8" STRIP SCREWED TO FRAME AFTER BOTTOM IS PLANKED

¼"×7½" STRINGER
½"×1¼" SPRUCE HEADER
SIDE PLANK 3/8" MAHOGANY
SEAM BATTENS 3/8"×1½" SPRUCE
KEEL BATTENS ¾"×2" SPRUCE
½"×1½" DK. SUPPORT FR.6
FRAMES 5/8" SPRUCE
SHORT BEAMS ½"×1½" or 5/8"×⅜"
BOTTOM PLANK 5/16"
FRAMES NO. 1,3-5&7 SHAPED AS SHOWN
2"
½"
2"

— WASP — No. 7 —

TOP OF BEAMS AT ℄
TOP OF BEAMS AT SIDE
SHEER LINE OR ℄ OR TOP OF BEAMS AT SIDE
TOP OF BEAMS AT SIDE
KNUCKLE OR CHINE
ACTUAL KNUCKLE OR CHINE
PROJECTED KNUCKLE

3¾"
3/8" = D.
¾" = D.
1⅛" = D.
5/16" = D.
15/16" = D.
1¼" = D.

0   1   2   3   4   5   6   7   8
2'2" 18" 18" 18" 16" 16" 16" 16"

17"

SCALE 1'
0   1   2 FT.

—WASP—
LENGTH 11'-10" BEAM 5'

E.G.M. 1932

PROJECTED KNUCKLE
TRANSOM CROWNED 3" IN 4'-6"

HEIGHTS ABOVE BASE			HALF-BREADTHS		
	TOP OF DECK	KNUCKLE & OF BOTTOM	KNUCKLE OR BOTTOM	TOP OF KNUCKLE	TOP OF DECK
1	1-6-3	0-11-3	0-9-4	1-1-4	1-3-6
2	1-5-7	0-8-1	0-6-4	1-8-2	1-11-1
3	1-5-2	0-5-7	0-4-7	2-1-0	2-3-2
4	1-4-5	0-4-4	0-4-0	2-4-0	2-5-4
5	1-4-1	0-6-3	0-5-4	2-5-3	2-6-1
6	1-3-5	0-5-3	0-4-6	2-5-6	2-5-5
7	1-3-1	0-4-2	0-3-7	2-5-6	2-4-6
8	1-2-5	0-3-1	0-3-1	2-5-6	2-3-3

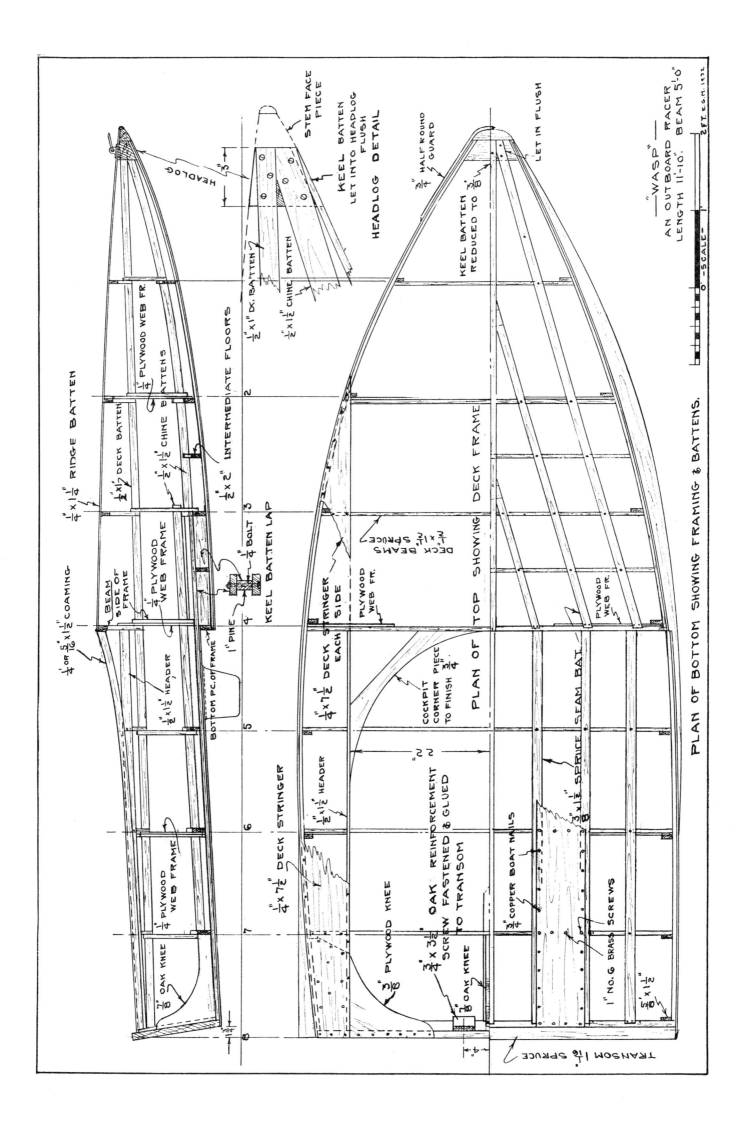

HEADLOG DETAIL

KEEL BATTEN
LET INTO HEADLOG
FLUSH

STEM FACE PIECE

½"×1" DK. BATTEN

½"×1½" CHINE BATTEN

¾" HALF ROUND GUARD

KEEL BATTEN
REDUCED TO ⅜"

LET IN FLUSH

HEADLOG

¼"×1¼" RIDGE BATTEN

PLYWOOD WEB FR.

½"×1" DECK BATTEN

¼" PLYWOOD WEB FRAME

½"×1½" CHINE BATTENS

½"×2" INTERMEDIATE FLOORS

¼"×1¼" BATTENS

2

KEEL BATTEN LAP

¼" BOLT

3

1" PINE

4

BEAM SIDE OF FRAME

⅝"×1½" COAMING

¼" OR ⁵⁄₁₆" PLYWOOD WEB FRAME

½"×1½" HEADER

BOTTOM PC. OF FRAME

DECK BEAMS ½"×1½" SPRUCE

PLYWOOD WEB FR.

¼"×7½" DECK STRINGER EACH SIDE

PLAN OF TOP SHOWING DECK FRAME

COCKPIT CORNER PIECE TO FINISH ⅜"

½"×1½" HEADER

2"

5

¼"×7½" DECK STRINGER

½"×1½" HEADER

6

¼" PLYWOOD WEB FRAME

⅝" OAK REINFORCEMENT FASTENED & GLUED

⅝" PLYWOOD KNEE

¾"×3½" OAK SCREW FASTENED TO TRANSOM

⅝" OAK KNEE

⅝" OAK KNEE

3"×1½" SPRUCE SEAM BAT.

¾" COPPER BOAT NAILS

1" NO.6 BRASS SCREWS

⅝"×1½"

7

8

2"

TRANSOM 1⅛" SPRUCE

PLAN OF BOTTOM SHOWING FRAMING & BATTENS.

"WASP"

AN OUTBOARD RACER

LENGTH 11'-10". BEAM 5'-0"

SCALE

2 FT. E.G.H. 1932

"Hornet," A Racing Hydroplane

AN OUTSTANDING 125 CLASS HYDROPLANE BY JOHN HACKER
Photo by permission of Mr. Hacker

THIS LITTLE HYDRO is intended for competition in the 125 and 151 class and the several intermediate local divisions. These boats have improved greatly since the *Margarete III* days, principally through the efforts of the racing associations. A hull-weight minimum has added greatly to their safety and practicability, and a nice appearing, highly enjoyable little craft has resulted. A price limit on the power plants in some classes has served further to popularize the type.

The modern trend has been incorporated in this plan, but without sacrifice of speed. With proper handling and a motor with real pep, she should be right out in front in real fast company. The driver has been placed as far forward as weight distribution will permit, as in the late Hacker craft. The boat illustrated is fourteen feet long, beam four feet eight inches, and with a 47 H. P. motor makes 40 miles per hour.

Construction features are diagonal planking (inside layer) and web frames; a combination providing maximum strength with a minimum of weight. Before starting construction it would be best to consult the racing association's latest rulings for the class in which you intend racing. It may be necessary to make minor changes in order to qualify, as the rules are frequently revised. The 125 class requires a watertight bulkhead not less than three feet from bow, bottom plank 3/8" or heavier, with sides not less than 5/16", and the deck must be at least 1/4" and able to stand the weight of one man. The motor is required to be under hatches and exhaust through the stern, and the boat in racing trim shall weigh not less than 750 pounds. There are other requirements, so that you can see the advisability of consulting the rule book. All official motorboat racing in this country and Canada is carried on under the jurisdiction of the American Power Boat Asso-

ciation, and its regulations may be found in its yearbook, which is best obtained through your local yacht or power-boat club. The address of the association is 17640 E. Nine Mile Rd., Eastpointe, Michigan 48021. No steam box is required in the construction of this boat.

The Lumber Order

Keel—2 pcs. 3/4" × 4"—7' hardwood.

Stem—1 3/4" natural crook or 1 pc. 1 3/4" × 10"—3'.

Frames—20 B. M. 3/4" thick, 5' and longer (some 6" or wider).

Battens and Clamp—4 pcs. 1/2" × 1 1/2"—16' and 2 pcs. 3/8" × 1 1/2" —16' spruce.

Planking—300 B. M. 3/16" × 5 1/2" S. 4 S., 30% in 16' lengths, use short pieces for diagonals.

Chine for'd—2 pcs. 7/8" × 2"—9' and 2 pcs. 3/4" × 1 1/4"—9'.

Chine aft—2 pcs. 1 1/2" × 1 1/2"—7'.

Transom—2 pcs. 3/4" × 9"—4' 6" mahogany.

Engine Stringers—2 pcs. 7/8" × 10"—12' spruce.

Engine Bed—2 pcs. 1 3/4" × 10"—4'.

Web Frames—3 pcs. 3/8" × 22"—3'—1/4" plywood.

Beams and Hatches—1 pc. 3/4" × 12"—12'.

Deck Battens—12 pcs. 1/4" × 1"—10'.

Deck—2 pcs. 1/4" × 10"—13' and 10 pcs. 1/4" × 6"—10'.

Seat Back—1 pc. 3/8" × 18"—3' 6" plywood.

Seat Bottom—1 pc. 3/8" × 16"—5' plywood.

Coaming—2 pcs. 3/8" × 6"—4' 6".

Windshield—1 pc. 1/8" × 14"—4' composition board.

Guards—2 pcs. 1" halfround—16'.

Step Fasure—1 pc. 1/2" × 8"—6' long.

The construction methods and details in the text of this book will apply closely here, and the following is intended to fill in the gaps and treat this craft individually.

To completely lay down this boat, though not necessary, should offer no difficulties, and you can then obtain rabbet and bearding line for stem not shown on detail; otherwise it must be cut after stem is set up. All frames in this case are placed on for'd side of station line, there being but little bevel aft and no separate frame floors, except on frame No. 1. This will place the moulding face to floor just opposite to Fig. No. 5, and this face will always be aft when setting up. The plywood webs on stations Nos. 3 and 9 should be cut to shape, placed on body plan, and frame assembled on top, then turn over and fasten into frames through plywood, using ¾″ brass screws. The web on frame No. 6 is on for'd side of frame, which will be up when assembling, so will be no different than fastening the corner gussets; these are omitted on web frames. Deck beams are assembled on frames Nos. 3, 6, and 9, and camber must be laid out separately for each; also for transom, as shown on lines drawing. No cross-bands are placed on the balance of the frames except on No. 1.

The inner or diagonal planking will butt against the transom, so a ¾″ frame must be fastened around it and ³⁄₁₆″ in from edge, as the outer or fore and aft planking ends flush with the aft side of transom, and deduct but ³⁄₁₆″ from transom for plank thickness instead of ⅜″ as for frames.

Stem detail is shown on page 69, and in case a natural crook is not available build up of two pieces, as in runabout *Tern*. In setting up this boat a slightly different procedure than usual is followed. A set-up stringer is cut from lines to shape of keel bottom, using a 2 × 6 or wider, or built up of two pieces joined at the step; allow for'd ends to project in a straight line almost to station No. 0. Frame stations and base line are marked on it and it is set up on edge and is levelled, using base line, plumbed and braced as in setting up a keel; see Fig. No. 10.

The ¾″ × 4″ keel pieces are placed on the stringer; the aft piece runs from ¾″ for'd of station No. 11 to station No. 6, and the for'd one from station No. 6 to just aft of station No. 1, as shown. The stem may be fitted to keel on the loft floor or by measuring from base line and frame stations on the stringer. In either case the stringer must be cut away a little for forefoot. Stem and keel should be fastened together on the bench, then replaced and stem plumbed and braced.

All frames notch over keel and numbers 9, 6, 3, 1, and transom are set up much as explained under "Setting Up" and shown in Fig. No. 10. Frame No. 1 straddles forefoot much as shown in detail for runabout *Sunray*. On Fig. No. 10 the ribbands are numbered, and in this case run a light one about ¾″ × 1½″ around topsides (marked No. 3) and on bottom run No. 1; the latter may be a straight edge aft of step. The intermediate frames are now fitted in place and the keel should be fastened to all frames with one 2″ No. 12 screw each side of stringer.

The clamp is fastened to each frame with one 1¼″ No. 8 screw and the aft chine is rabbeted from a single piece, as it is almost square. Forward the chine is in two pieces and is laid out as described under "Chine and the Keel Batten." The for'd chine cuts through the step frame and the inner

piece is covered later by the ½″ fasure shown in step detail, the outer chine extends through fasure. The ⅜″ × 1½″ side batten is notched into frames, as shown, and fastened to each with a 1″ No. 8 screw.

Engine stringers are best fitted now and their spread will be governed to suit motor installed; the lightening holes are bored at each end with an expansion bit and sawed out between. This is a good time to run the shaft line, marking it on engine stringer and keel and noting the distance down from transom, but hole through keel cannot be cut yet.

The balance of the beams should now be fitted; spring a batten down centreline of beams from stem to transom and obtain crown of these from it, and place a ¾″ × 1″ support from centre of beam to frame floor below at stations Nos. 1 and 2.

Side planking is next and the inner layer is laid diagonally, about forty-five degrees from horizontal; choose the poorest planking for this. Start forward, glue to clamp, chine, batten, and frames and fasten to these same members with ¾″ copper wire nails, clinch where too long. When doing so keep in mind that outer skin must fasten into these same members. See that plank does not pull hollow spots in side battens between frames for'd. The whole should now be painted with marine glue and a sheet of thin muslin stretched over it, ironing it out much as stretching canvas over the deck.

Start fore-and-aft plank with the chine plank, paint well with marine glue before each plank is put on and fasten before glue sets. The hull is not caulked and depends for watertightness upon the glue and muslin; if too thick the glue will keep plank surfaces apart between fastenings, and if too thin will not serve its purpose. If a varnish finish is desired the powdered cold-water glue will not do, as it stains the surface. Use 1″ No. 6 screws in frames, chine, stem, and transom, with heads sunk just below the surface, and between frames fasten with ⅝″ copper tacks, as shown, and clinch against a hold-on (see "The Dory Lap").

The outer face of each plank should be hand-planed on the bench, as on account of flush fastening most of the smoothing will have to be done with a large flat file used on tack heads, and scraper and sand-paper.

After boat is turned over the shaft hole should be cut through keel and the ½″ × 1½″ batten fitted about halfway between keel and chine. The bottom is planked in same manner as topsides; complete that portion aft of step first (both layers) and then the diagonal plank for'd. The ½″ fasure is fitted against step, as shown, and the fore-and-aft planking is then finished. Use copper nails in bottom battens and clinch.

The deck planks are fastened to seam battens with ¾″ copper boat nails clinched underneath. Sometimes the centre or king plank is made of some light-colored wood, such as white cedar or spruce, and the balance of red cedar or some other dark wood. Another nice effect may be had by using covering boards and making them and king plank dark and balance light, or vice versa. The two pieces ¼″ × 10″—13′ are for each side of deck, as shown, and the diagonal hatch planking is optional.

A patent metal shaft log is shown, but a wooden one, such as shown for *Tern*, may be used. If babbitt is used in strut allow 3/16″ all around and drill at least four anchor holes through the barrel; a turned bushing is often used, in which case wall or bushing should be 1/8″. In making strut pattern follow same procedure as described for *Tern*.

If the boat is to qualify for competition in the 125 cubic-inch class a 1/4″ plywood bulkhead should be substituted for the web frame on station No. 3, in which case the rudder must be moved aft a few inches. The deck aft should be left until strut, steering gear and tank are installed.

Strut, rudder and stem details are shown under *Tern*, page 69.

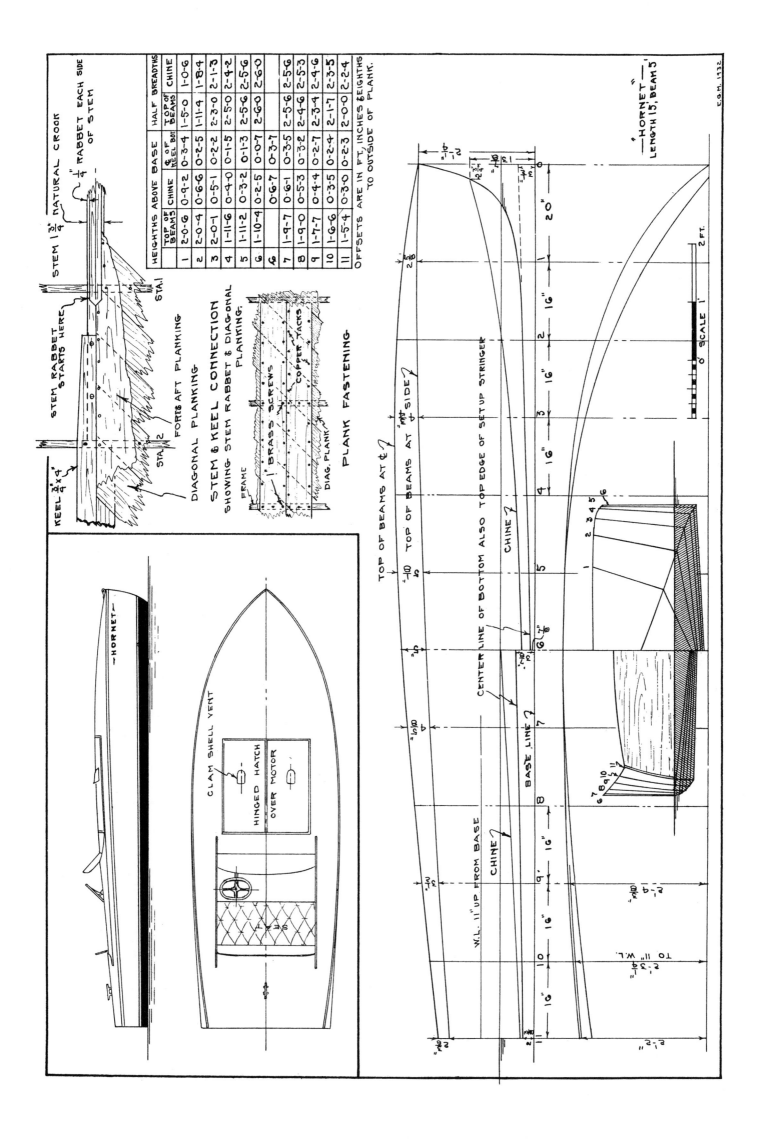

STEM 1¾" NATURAL CROOK

STEM 1¾"

STEM RABBET STARTS HERE

FORE & AFT PLANKING.

KEEL ¾" x 4"

STA. 1

STA. 2

DIAGONAL PLANKING.

STEM & KEEL CONNECTION
SHOWING- STEM RABBET & DIAGONAL PLANKING.

BRASS SCREWS

COPPER TACKS

FRAME

DIAG. PLANK

PLANK FASTENING.

¼" RABBET EACH SIDE OF STEM

HEIGHTS ABOVE BASE			HALF BREADTHS	
	TOP OF BEAMS	CHINE	₵ OF KEEL BOT	TOP OF BEAMS	CHINE
1	2-0-6	0-9-2	0-3-4	1-5-0	1-0-6
2	2-0-4	0-6-6	0-2-5	1-11-4	1-8-4
3	2-0-1	0-5-1	0-2-2	2-3-0	2-1-3
4	1-11-6	0-4-0	0-1-5	2-5-0	2-4-2
5	1-11-2	0-3-2	0-1-3	2-5-6	2-5-6
6	1-10-4	0-2-5	0-0-7	2-6-0	2-6-0
6		0-6-7	0-3-7		
7	1-9-7	0-6-1	0-3-5	2-5-6	2-5-6
8	1-9-0	0-5-3	0-3-2	2-4-6	2-5-3
9	1-7-7	0-4-4	0-2-7	2-3-4	2-4-6
10	1-6-6	0-3-5	0-2-4	2-1-7	2-3-5
11	1-5-4	0-3-0	0-2-3	2-0-0	2-2-4

OFFSETS ARE IN FT., INCHES &EIGHTHS TO OUTSIDE OF PLANK.

—HORNET—
LENGTH 13, BEAM 5

E.G.M. 1932.

—HORNET—

CLAM SHELL VENT

HINGED HATCH

OVER MOTOR

SEAT

TOP OF BEAMS AT ₵

TOP OF BEAMS AT ₵ SIDE

CHINE

CENTER LINE OF BOTTOM ALSO TOP EDGE OF SETUP STRINGER

BASE LINE

W.L. 11" UP FROM BASE

CHINE

TO 11" W.L.

SCALE

0   SCALE 1'   2 FT.

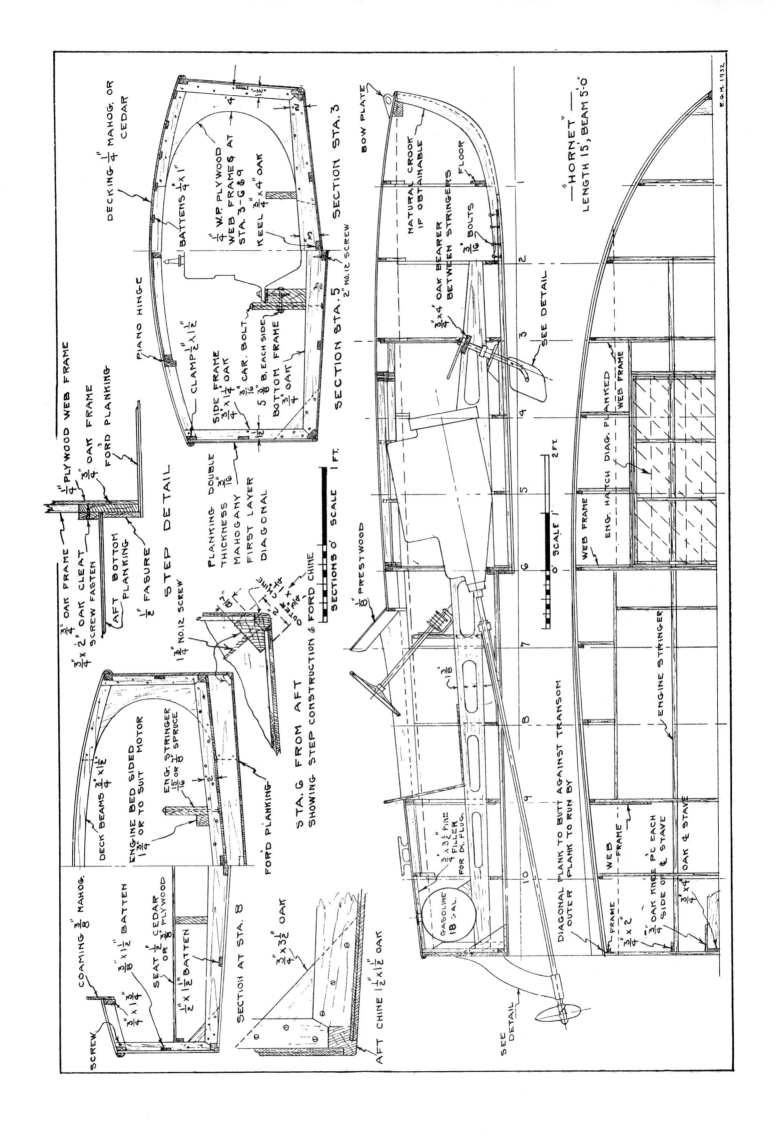

"HORNET"
LENGTH 15', BEAM 5'-0"

E.G.H. 1932

"Tern,"
An 18′ Runabout

THE MOST POPULAR motorboat of today, aside from the outboards, is doubtless the small inboard runabout, and the first thought regarding any particular design is generally, How fast will it go? Speed is dependent principally upon weight and horsepower, provided, of course, that the proper hull form has been chosen for the job on hand. The hull lines of *Tern* are those of the typical high-speed runabout, with its long buttocks aft and straight chine. With a motor weighing about 300 pounds and developing 45 H. P., a speed close to 30 miles may be expected. There are several motors of 15 to 20 H. P. which should drive the boat about 20 miles per hour. The forward driving position and complete accessibility of motor are desirable features of the arrangement.

An automobile motor offers the only power available to many, and if a suitable motor is properly installed and conservatively used it will give satisfaction. Some provision must be made for cooling the cylinder oil. A marine clutch and reverse should be installed and a water-cooled manifold is desirable. A marine propeller or an electric generator are about the toughest consignments for any motor, as, unlike an automobile, there is no let-up but a continual full-power drag. For this reason when doping out a wheel, rate the motor at about 60 per cent of its maximum power and it will still have the hardest job of its career.

The Lumber Order

Stem—1 pc. 1¾″ × 9″—3′.
Keel and Keel Batten—1 pc. 1″ × 1¾″—16′, 1 pc. ¾″ × 3½″—16′.
Forefoot—1 pc. 1¾″ × 10″ N.—4′.
Frames—30 B. M. ¾″ × 8″ or wider and 8 B. M. 1¹⁄₁₆″ × 6″ or wider.
Chine—2 pcs. ¾″ × 2¼″—18′ and 2 pcs. ¾″ × 1⅝″—18′.

Seam Battens—16 pcs. ⅜″ × 1½″—19′.
Sheer Battens—2 pcs. ¾″ × 1½″—19′.
Clamp—2 pcs. ½″ × 1½″—19′.
Shelf—2 pcs. 1½″ × 4″—7′.
Planking—Bottom—4 pcs. ½″ × 8″—18′ and 6 pcs. ½″ × 6″—18′.
Planking—Topsides—8 pcs. ½″ × 6″—19′ and 2 pcs. ½″ × 8″—19′.
Planking—Transom—3 pcs. ¾″ × 8″—4′ 6″.
Engine Stringers—2 pcs. 1¼″ × 6″—10′.
Engine Bed—2 pcs. 2¼″ × 8″—4′ 1″.
Shaft Log—1 pc. 3½″ × 6″—2′ 6″ (or use metal log).
Deck Beams and Deck Frame—2 pcs. ⅞″ × 12″—5′, 1 pc. 1¾″ × 8″—5′ and 6 pcs. 1¹⁄₁₆″ × 1¾″—4′.
Deck—2 pcs. ½″ × 10″—15′ and 75 B. M. ½″ × 3″ T. and G. (includes cockpit flooring).
Coaming—Aft—2 pcs. ½″ × 4″—5′ and 1 pc. ½″ × 8″—5′, for'd 2 pcs. ½″ × 8″—5′.
Bulkheads—1 pc. ½″ × 30″—5′ and 1 pc. ½″ × 32″—5′ plywood.
Seat Backs—1 pc. ½″ × 24″—5′ and 1 pc. ½″ × 18″—4′ plywood.
Seat Bottoms—1 pc. ⅜″ × 24″—5′ and 1 pc. ⅜″ × 18″—5′ plywood.
Seat Fronts—1 pc. ½″ × 10″—10′.
Guards—2 pcs. ¾″ × 1¼″—19′ and 2 pcs. ¾″ × 1¼″—6′.
Breasthook—1 pc. 2″ × 6″—18″.

Heavier straight-grain lumber may be substituted for plywood seat, backs, and bottoms. Steaming is advisable for the for'd ends of the garboard and one or two planks next to it and also some of the planks near the sheer.

The construction methods and details in the text of this book will apply closely here, and the following is intended to fill in the gaps and treat this craft individually.

The plans have been so drawn that the boat can be constructed from the body-plan lines only, but as explained elsewhere the time spent in completely lofting the boat will be well invested.

The boat is erected upside down as in Fig. No. 9, and as the sheerline is straight we will use it as a set-up line, fastening the cross-bands to each frame above sheer mark, with bottom edge on same as in Fig. No. 5. For this reason each frame side piece should be made two or three inches long. You will note that all frames are on the for'd side of the station line, and do not change at midship as is generally the case. Frames Nos. 1 to 5 will be assembled as in Fig. No. 5 with moulding face up, but Nos. 6, 7, and 8 will have the moulding face down against the floor, and floors and gussets fastened to for'd side of frame. This, you will note, places the entire after-frames on for'd side of station line, as in the plans. Tack a temporary floor at frame No. 7, putting the permanent one in after shaft log is in place. Frames Nos. 1 and 2 are notched over forefoot, as shown in small detail for *Sunray*, an outboard runabout. After frames Nos. 4 and 6 are assembled, use them as templates for marking the plywood bulkheads, which will save much fitting later.

The erecting stringers (Fig. No. 9) are set up three feet six inches apart, outside to outside, and with a fore-and-aft slope of seven inches in seventeen feet eight inches to place boat on an even keel; see lines drawings. A glance at *Sunbeam* will show position of stringer and method of attaching transom to it. The transom and each frame is, of course, set up plumb and not in this case square up and down from the stringers.

The keel batten will scarf into forefoot, as shown, and is fastened to each frame with two 2″ No. 12 screws. Fasten keel to keel batten, as explained in text, and a special effort should be made to obtain a tight glue joint in the vicinity of shaft hole. I would use clamps here and leave until glue is well set. The chines follow and the outer chine tapers to about ½″ × ⅞″ at stem.

As the engine stringers are through-bolted to the frame floors they should be put in now. Ascertain from motor the distance apart the engine beds should be, and place the stringers accordingly. The chine and keel will hold the frames rigidly in place, and all ribbands, etc., may be removed to make things more get-at-able. Slip the engine stringers in from forward and fit them to floors. A cleat nailed on frames Nos. 3 and 8, to fit them against, will aid greatly in placing them. Now is the time to cut shaft hole through keel and install shaft log; see "Shaft Log and Engine Beds." By removing the cross-bands on frames Nos. 6 and 4 it should be possible to slip in the two plywood bulkheads. They will have to be fitted around the engine stringers and fastened to frame with 3d galvanized nails (also glue).

Fasten plank to frames with 1¼″ galvanized boat nails and to seam battens with 1″ copper boat nails clinched inside, or with ¾″ brass screws. At least two streaks of side planking next to chine must be put on before boat is turned over. If topsides are to be varnished, use screws here entirely and plug.

The boat may now be turned over, the cross-bands removed and refastened, one at a time, lower down to clear the clamp. (See "Deck Beams, etc.") The ¾″ × 1½″ sheer batten should be fitted next, and is shown let into the frames plumb, as this eliminates all twist and edge set; screw-fasten to frames, using one 1½″ No. 10 screw in each frame. The clamp, deck beams, and the shelves at side of cockpit must be put in before planking can be completed. The sheer battens should be screw-fastened into the cockpit shelves and the ends of shelves well fastened through deck beams, thus tying the boat well together at these points. Nail through sheer batten into beam ends and screw-fasten ends to frame. The two pieces, ½″ × 10″, ordered for decking are intended for each side of cockpits, and will extend from transom forward of frame No. 2.

It will be much easier to install gas tanks, sheaves for tiller line, and even the rudder and strut, before the aft deck is laid. The hinged hatches over motor should be bound with brass, as shown in detail.

A pattern must be made of the strut and it must be split fore and aft on centreline, or *A–A* in the sketch. This is best done by making leg of pattern of two ⅜″ pieces dowelled together, with half of palm and barrel mounted on each piece. The moulder can then pull each half of pattern out of the sand. Core prints, etc., will be taken care of at the foundry, unless the builder is familiar with pattern work and makes them himself. In making the pattern, remember that bronze shrinks 3/16″ per foot in cooling. Bolt strut through a 1½″ × 7½″ oak block, run well out each side of centreline, and screw-fastened to planking.

The rudder may be made as per detail or else cast from a pattern with a Tobin bronze stock cast in the blade.

The engine beds are fitted between bulkheads and bolted to stringers with ⅜″ carriage bolts. The engine installation is covered in the text matter, and the balance of the boat needs little explanation.

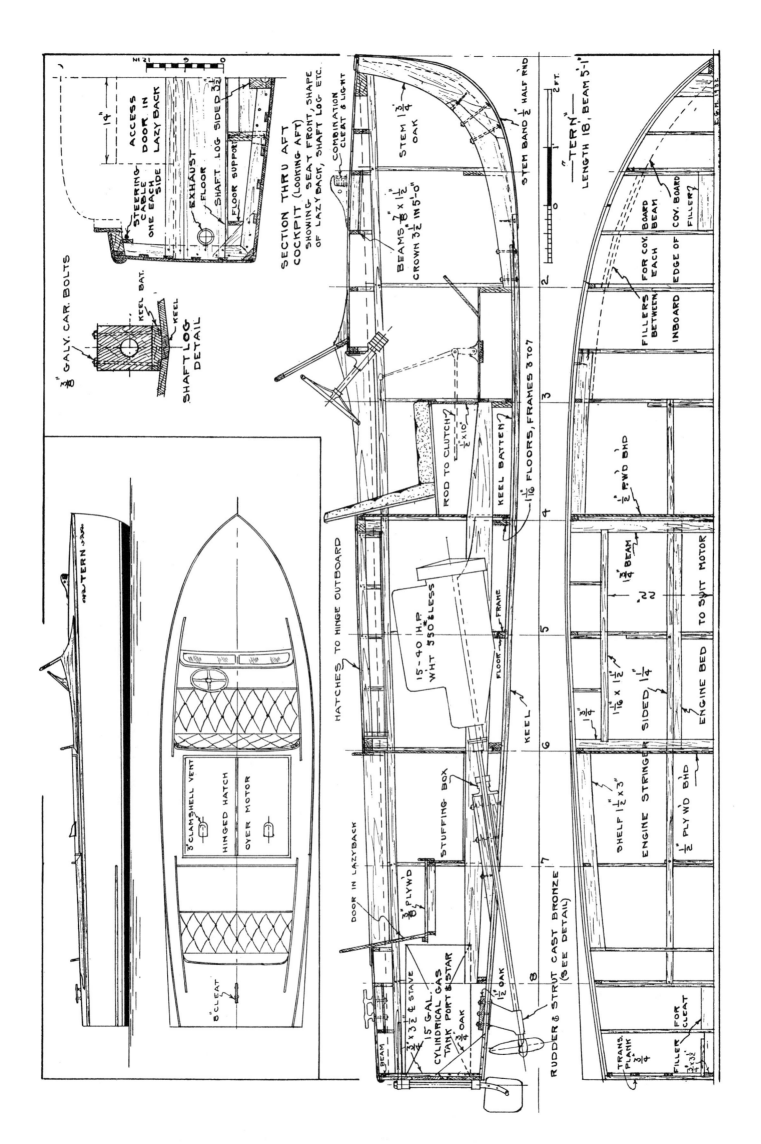

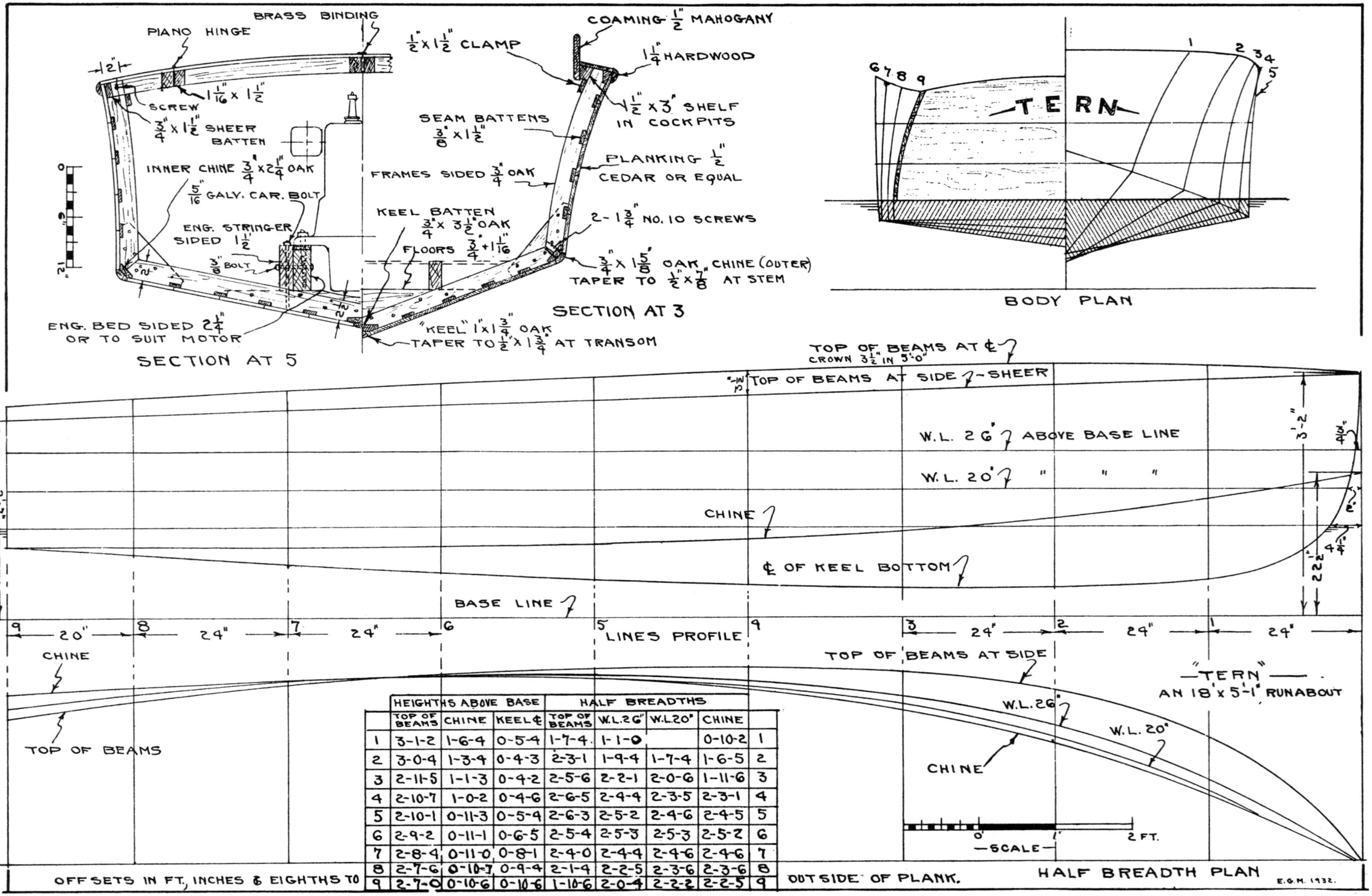
BRASS BINDING
PIANO HINGE
$1\frac{1}{16}" \times 1\frac{1}{2}"$
SCREW
$\frac{3}{4}" \times 1\frac{1}{2}"$ SHEER BATTEN
INNER CHINE $\frac{3}{4}" \times 2\frac{1}{4}"$ OAK
$\frac{5}{16}"$ GALV. CAR. BOLT
ENG. STRINGER SIDED $1\frac{1}{2}"$
$\frac{3}{8}"$ BOLT
ENG. BED SIDED $2\frac{1}{4}"$ OR TO SUIT MOTOR
SECTION AT 5
$\frac{1}{2}" \times 1\frac{1}{2}"$ CLAMP
COAMING $\frac{1}{2}"$ MAHOGANY
$1\frac{1}{4}"$ HARDWOOD
$1\frac{1}{2}" \times 3"$ SHELF IN COCKPITS
SEAM BATTENS $\frac{3}{8}" \times 1\frac{1}{2}"$
PLANKING $\frac{1}{2}"$ CEDAR OR EQUAL
FRAMES SIDED $\frac{3}{4}"$ OAK
KEEL BATTEN $\frac{3}{4}" \times 3\frac{1}{2}"$ OAK
FLOORS $\frac{3}{4}" + 1\frac{1}{16}"$
2-$1\frac{3}{4}"$ NO. 10 SCREWS
$\frac{3}{4}" \times 1\frac{5}{8}"$ OAK CHINE (OUTER) TAPER TO $\frac{1}{2}" \times \frac{7}{8}"$ AT STEM
"KEEL" $1" \times 1\frac{3}{4}"$ OAK TAPER TO $\frac{1}{2}" \times 1\frac{3}{4}"$ AT TRANSOM
SECTION AT 3
TERN
BODY PLAN
TOP OF BEAMS AT ℄
CROWN $3\frac{1}{2}"$ IN 5'-0"
TOP OF BEAMS AT SIDE — SHEER
W.L. 26" ABOVE BASE LINE
W.L. 20" " " "
CHINE
℄ OF KEEL BOTTOM
BASE LINE
LINES PROFILE
20"
24"
2'-7"
TOP OF BEAMS AT SIDE
"TERN"
AN 18' x 5'-1" RUNABOUT
W.L. 26"
W.L. 20"
TOP OF BEAMS
SCALE
2 FT.
HALF BREADTH PLAN
E.G.M. 1932.

OFFSETS IN FT, INCHES & EIGHTHS TO OUTSIDE OF PLANK.

	HEIGHTHS ABOVE BASE			HALF BREADTHS				
	TOP OF BEAMS	CHINE	KEEL ℄	TOP OF BEAMS	W.L.26"	W.L.20"	CHINE	
1	3-1-2	1-6-4	0-5-4	1-7-4	1-1-0		0-10-2	1
2	3-0-4	1-3-4	0-4-3	2-3-1	1-9-4	1-7-4	1-6-5	2
3	2-11-5	1-1-3	0-4-2	2-5-6	2-2-1	2-0-6	1-11-6	3
4	2-10-7	1-0-2	0-4-6	2-6-5	2-4-4	2-3-5	2-3-1	4
5	2-10-1	0-11-3	0-5-4	2-6-3	2-5-2	2-4-6	2-4-5	5
6	2-9-2	0-11-1	0-6-5	2-5-4	2-5-3	2-5-3	2-5-2	6
7	2-8-4	0-11-0	0-8-1	2-4-0	2-4-4	2-4-6	2-4-6	7
8	2-7-6	0-10-7	0-9-4	2-1-4	2-2-5	2-3-6	2-3-6	8
9	2-7-0	0-10-6	0-10-6	1-10-6	2-0-4	2-2-2	2-2-5	9

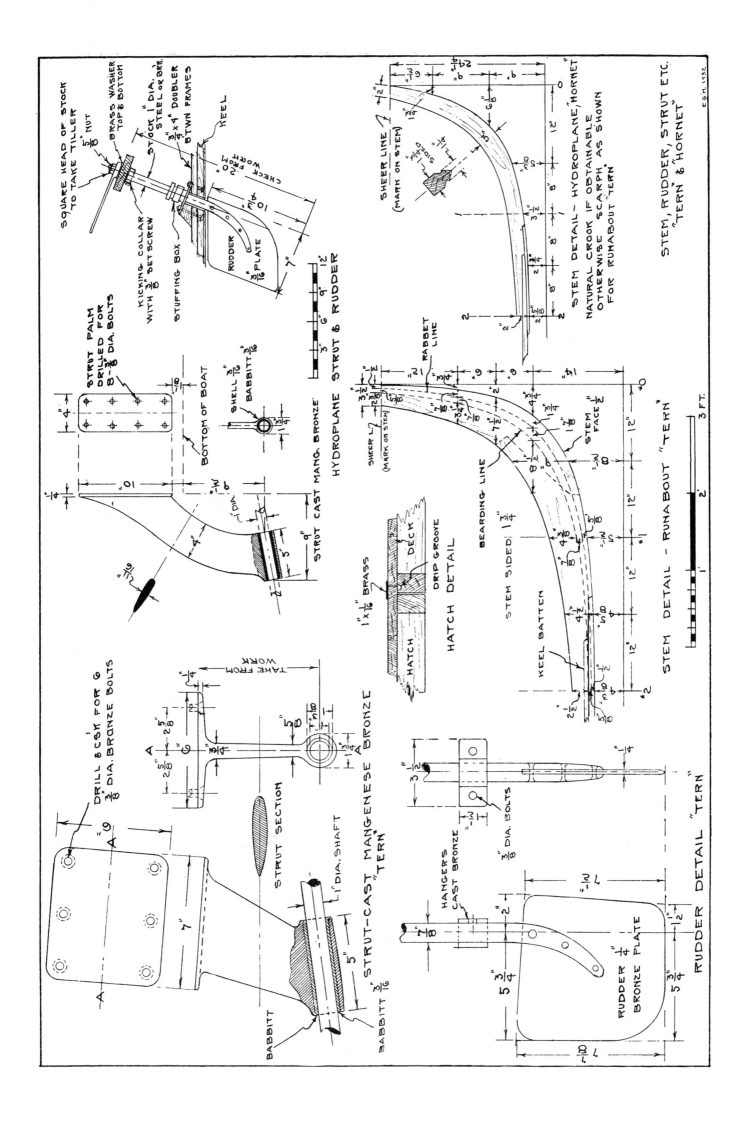

STEM, RUDDER, STRUT ETC.
"TERN" & "HORNET"

E.G.H. 1432.

STEM DETAIL – HYDROPLANE, "HORNET"
NATURAL CROOK IF OBTAINABLE
OTHERWISE SCARPH AS SHOWN
FOR RUNABOUT "TERN"

STEM DETAIL – RUNABOUT "TERN"

HATCH DETAIL

HYDROPLANE STRUT & RUDDER

STRUT-CAST MANGENESE BRONZE
"TERN"

RUDDER DETAIL "TERN"

"Truant,"
A Simplified Sailer

THIS IS THE smallest of the sailers shown in this book; also the simplest and most easily constructed. It is twelve feet six inches long with a beam of five feet, which is about as small as is practical for a two-man crew. The small cockpit and wide side deck, as in Ted Geary's *Flattee*, make it practically non-sinkable, although, of course, as in any centreboarder, not non-capsizable. The object in this design has been a class or afternoon sailboat that can be built at the absolute zero in cash expenditure. The illustration is of a *Flattee*, a boat of very similar appearance and whose plans are shown elsewhere in this book.

In keeping cost to the absolute minimum, hoops and lacing replace track and slides, on mast and boom; and the simple gaff jaw replaces the gooseneck fitting. The dagger board requires no blocks or gear, and being of wood may be made by the builder without resort to machine shop or outside help. The object throughout has been to make it as inexpensive and as simple to construct as could be hoped for in any sailboat. The economies outlined above are, of course, optioned with the builder. No steam box is required.

The Lumber Order

Side Plank—2 pcs. ½″ × 14″—13′ or 4 pcs. 8″ wide.
Bottom Plank—2 pcs. ½″ × 10″—13′, 2 pcs. ½″ × 10″—11′, 2 pcs. ½″ × 10″—10′.
Frames—16 B. M. ¾″ × 6″ or wider, 5′ long and up.
Transom—1 pc. 1¹⁄₁₆″ × 14″ N. or 2 pcs. 8″ wide—4′.
Stem—1 pc. 1¾″ × 6″—18″, 1 pc. 1¼″ × 2″—18″.

Dagger Board Trunk—1 pc. ¾″ × 10″—7′.
Clamp and Chine—4 pcs. ½″ × 1½″—13′.
Beams—1 pc. ¾″ × 12″—12′.
Cockpit Stringer—1 pc. ¾″ × 1¾″—9′.
Breasthook and Mast Partner—1 pc. 1¾″ × 8″—2′ 6″.
Decking—60 B. M. ½″ × 3″ T. and G.
Guard—2 pcs. 1″ halfround—13′.
Trim and Coaming—2 pcs. ½″ × 8″—6′.
Floor Boards—6 pcs. ½″ × 4″—5′.
Spars—1 pc. 2½″ × 2½″—18′ and 1 pc. 1¾″ × 1¾″—9′ spruce.
Rudder—1 pc. 1¹⁄₁₆″ × 14″—2′ 6″, 1 pc. ½″ × 4″—2′ oak.
Chafing Battens—4 pcs. ½″ × 1″—11′ and 2 pcs. ½″ × 1″—6′.
Skeg—1 pc. 1¹⁄₁₆″ × 6″—6′.
Dagger Board—1 pc. 1″ × 14″—3′ 6″.

The construction methods and details in the text of this book will apply closely here, and the following is intended to fill in the gaps and treat this craft individually.

This boat is built very much as one would construct a skiff. The side boards are first sawed to shape, with each frame station marked as per plan, the stem and transom worked out, and frames at stations Nos. 3 and 5 assembled. Fasten a cross-band near top of these frames as in Fig. No. 6, also a cross brace to keep from racking. As the bottom has the same deadrise or shape throughout, one of the bottom pieces will serve as a pattern for all the frame floors, and the same applies to deck beams and top of transom. The ½" × 1½" notches for the chine should be cut in frames Nos. 3 and 5 now; the bevels of sides of these frames may be closely obtained from the deck-framing plan.

To prevent splitting, screw-fasten a ¾" × 2" cleat up and down just aft of transom and outside of side boards, and allow ends to project on each side of board two or three inches. The sides are stood on edge and stem fastened between them. A rope is passed around aft ends on for'd side of the above-mentioned cleats and ends of side board are pulled together until frame No. 3 can be fastened in place, the same process is followed until frame No. 5 and transom are in place. As you bend the plank around the frames slip a little piece of ½" stuff in chine notch to relieve strain on the plank edge and forestall any splits. Use 4d galvanized nails in frames and 6d in stem and transom, if of soft wood; use thick paint and a small thread of cotton between at transom and stem. (See "Caulking.")

The chine strip should now be bevelled at for'd end to fit the stem, and slipped into the frame notches and butted against transom; fasten through plank into stem and frames with 6d galvanized wire nails. Put glue between chine and plank and fasten through plank with 1" No. 8 screws, or use 1¼" copper boat nails clinched inside. Be sure and pull the two tightly together everywhere, using a clamp if need be.

Place the boat at a convenient height for working on the deck frame, and fair up top edge of sheer or side planks. The balance of the frames are now put in. I would fit the floor piece first; as before mentioned, they are all the same shape; tack it in place and fit and bevel the side members, carefully marking the laps, and fasten the whole together on the bench. Use two 1½" No. 10 screws in each lap with glue between. The frame can then be replaced, the deck beam fitted, the frame again removed and beam fastened to it.

The dagger-board trunk is built as shown, leaving a slot one and one-sixteenth inches by fourteen and one-half inches for the board, or one-half inch by fourteen and one-half inches if a metal board is used; put thick paint and cotton between joints and fasten sides to end pieces with 1½" No. 10 screws; notch ends for beams and frames and fasten in place.

The bottom is next. Cut out of plank for dagger-board slot and put thick paint and a thin thread of cotton around edges of trunk, across transom, and all around edge of side boards. Fasten around trunk and transom with 1½" No. 8 screws; use 4d galvanized nails into frames and at edges into chine piece and side boards, spacing them about 2½" and staggering. Provide a one-sixteenth inch seam between bottom planks for caulking.

While still bottom up the skeg should be put on; plane a flat spot one and one-sixteenth inches wide down centreline, caulk and putty the seam and fit skeg, both forward and aft of dagger-board slot. Fasten where not too deep to each frame with a large galvanized nail, and to transom with the ¾" × 1¹⁄₁₆" oak strip shown.

Turn the boat over, put in the keel battens, fitting them between the frames, fasten through plank into skeg, using 6d galvanized nails; also fit mast step, securely fastening it to frames and through plank from outside. The clamp is fastened to frames with 4d galvanized nails; the intermediate beams, breasthook, mast partner, cockpit framing and fillers follow. The brace shown at station No. 3 should be about ¾" × 2", and one is fitted each side of frame and well fastened. Before deck is laid, the mast hole and the step mortise should be cut; stretch a line from top of transom to sheerline on stem and rake the mast aft three inches in five feet from square off this line. Mast is shown square from deck down, as it is easier to wedge than if round.

The deck is laid and canvased in usual manner, using 4d galvanized nails into beams, etc. Canvas is turned down all around edges and covered at stem by the stem face piece and along sides and across transom by the guard and inside cockpit by the fasure.

Chain plates should go on before guards, and the best method of fastening them is explained under *Curlew*. A flat face three-fourths inch wide should be left at top of stem face for the jib-stay chain plate, or else install a stem band and fasten to it as in *Curlew*. Rudder and dagger-board are each shown made of one piece, but narrower stuff glued together will serve just as well. The dagger-board may be of steel, but though thinner it will offer more resistance than the stream-lined wood board.

Either much or little may be spent on the rig; as shown, little expenditure is required. A serviceable mast hoop can be made from ¼" copper tubing; flatten and lap the ends to get a rivet through them, round off a bit and bind the joint with tape, which should then be shellacked; fasten to sail at this point.

The breasthook as ordered is 1¾" thick, so a piece should be glued to it to bring it to the specified thickness shown in plan.

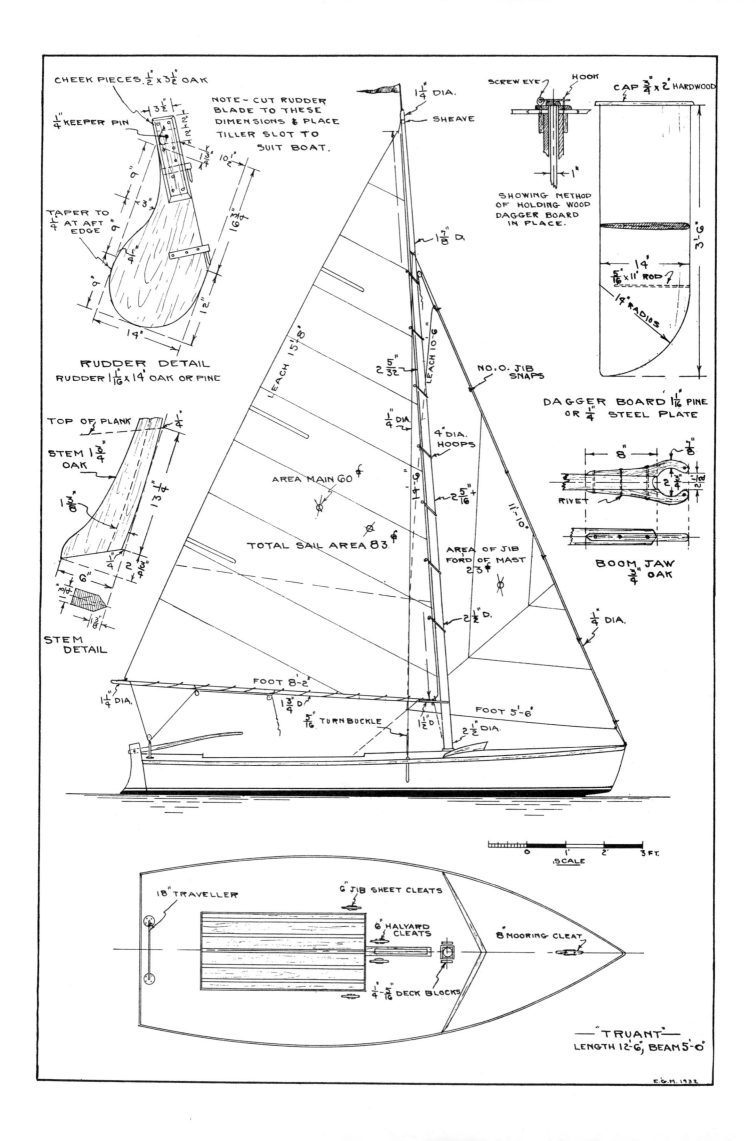

CHEEK PIECES $\frac{1}{2}$" x $3\frac{1}{2}$" OAK

NOTE- CUT RUDDER BLADE TO THESE DIMENSIONS & PLACE TILLER SLOT TO SUIT BOAT.

$\frac{1}{4}$" KEEPER PIN

TAPER TO $\frac{1}{4}$" AT AFT EDGE

RUDDER DETAIL
RUDDER $1\frac{1}{16}$" x 14" OAK OR PINE

SCREW EYE   HOOK

SHOWING METHOD OF HOLDING WOOD DAGGER BOARD IN PLACE.

CAP $\frac{3}{4}$" x 2" HARDWOOD

$\frac{5}{16}$" x 11" ROD

14"

3'-6"

14" RADIUS

DAGGER BOARD $1\frac{1}{16}$" PINE OR $\frac{1}{4}$" STEEL PLATE

TOP OF PLANK

STEM $1\frac{3}{4}$" OAK

STEM DETAIL

LEACH 15'-8"

LEACH 10'-6"

$1\frac{1}{4}$" DIA.

SHEAVE

$1\frac{7}{8}$" D.

NO. O. JIB SNAPS

$2\frac{5}{32}$"

$\frac{1}{4}$" DIA.

4" DIA. HOOPS

AREA MAIN 60 ☐

TOTAL SAIL AREA 83 ☐

$2\frac{5}{16}$"+

11'-10"

AREA OF JIB FORD OF MAST 23 ☐

$2\frac{1}{2}$" D.

$\frac{1}{4}$" DIA.

BOOM JAW OAK

RIVET

8"

FOOT 8'-2"

$1\frac{3}{4}$" D.

$\frac{5}{16}$" TURNBUCKLE

$1\frac{1}{2}$" D.

FOOT 5'-6"

$2\frac{1}{2}$" DIA.

$1\frac{1}{4}$" DIA.

SCALE
0   1'   2'   3 FT.

18" TRAVELLER

6" JIB SHEET CLEATS

6" HALYARD CLEATS

8" MOORING CLEAT

$\frac{1}{4}$" - $\frac{5}{16}$" DECK BLOCKS

"TRUANT"
LENGTH 12'-6", BEAM 5'-0"

E.G.M. 1932

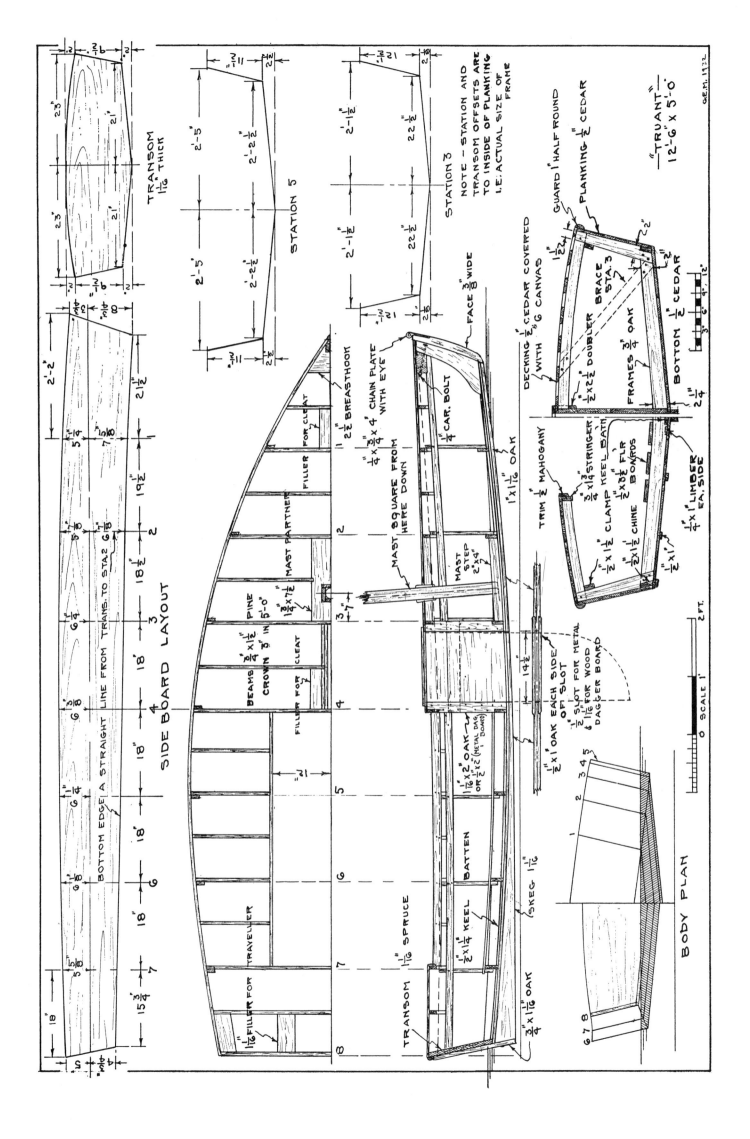

"Curlew,"
A Centreboard Sloop

FIRST PLACE IN the sailboat field is doubtless held by the small centreboard sloop, for it provides most of us with the means of enjoying one of the world's finest sports. It is inexpensive to build, easily cared for, and as it requires in competition quick thinking and handling is the ideal tutor for the young sailor.

This particular design offers a good, safe afternoon sailboat, with moderate rig and is simple to construct and easily handled. Unless ballasted it will not sink, and the ample freeboard and beam should add greatly to its seaworthiness. The hull shape possesses most of the advantages of the round-bottom boat with little of its difficult construction, and has proven very satisfactory in several of the author's magazine "How to Builds" and other designs. The illustration is of a smaller edition of *Curlew*; the hull shape is the same but the new design has been lengthened and partly decked over, as would befit a larger boat. Considering the expense and labor entailed, it should return large dividends in health and recreation.

The Lumber Order

Skeg or Keel—1 pc. $1\frac{1}{16}$" × 10"—6'.
Stem—1 pc. 2" × 9"—3' and 1 pc. $1\frac{1}{4}$" × 4"—2' 6".
Frames—30 B. M. $\frac{3}{4}$" × 8" or wider, 4' long and up.
Transom—1 pc. $1\frac{1}{4}$" × 18"—4' 4" or 2 pcs. 10" wide.
Plank—Bottom—2 pcs. $\frac{5}{8}$" × 10"—15', 2 pcs. $\frac{5}{8}$" × 10"—13', and 2 pcs. $\frac{5}{8}$" × 8"—12'.
Plank—Bilge—2 pcs. $\frac{5}{8}$" × 10"—16' and 2 pcs. $\frac{5}{8}$" × 12"—16'.
Plank—Topsides—2 pcs. $\frac{5}{8}$" × 12"—16' 6", or use dory lap and 2 pcs. $\frac{5}{8}$" × 8"—16', and 2 pcs. $\frac{5}{8}$" × 6"—16' 6".
Centreboard Trunk—1 pc. $\frac{3}{4}$" × 12"—9' and 1 pc. $\frac{3}{4}$" × 10"—9'.
Centreboard Trunk Cheek Piece—1 pc. $\frac{3}{4}$" × 4"—9'.

Chines—2 pcs. $\frac{1}{2}$" × 6"—8' and 2 pcs. $\frac{1}{2}$" × 6"—7'.
Deck Beams—1 pc. $\frac{3}{4}$" × 12"—6'.
Mast Partner and Breasthook—1 pc. 2" N. × 10"—3'.
Mast Step—1 pc. 2" × 4"—18".
Cockpit Stringers—1 pc. $\frac{3}{4}$" × 6"—9'.
Decking—2 pcs. $\frac{1}{2}$" × 12"—13' Cov. Board or side members, and 30 B. M. $\frac{1}{2}$" T. and G.
Floor Boards—6 pcs. $\frac{1}{2}$" × 4"—8'.
Cockpit Coaming—2 pcs. $\frac{1}{2}$" × 6"—10', 1 pc. $\frac{1}{2}$" × 6"—6', and 1 pc. $\frac{1}{2}$" × 8"—4'.
Seats—2 pcs. $\frac{3}{4}$" × 12"—9' and 2 pcs. $\frac{3}{4}$" × 6"—7'.
Spars—1 pc. 3" × 3"—22' and 1 pc. $2\frac{1}{2}$" × $2\frac{1}{2}$"—12' spruce.
Rudder—1 pc. $1\frac{1}{16}$" × 10"—4' 6".
Guards—2 pcs. 1" halfround 17'.
Bottom Battens, Clamps, etc., from planking scraps.
Trunk Stiffeners—2 pcs. $\frac{1}{2}$" × 3"—2' oak.

The construction methods and details in the text of this book will apply closely here, and the following is intended to fill in the gaps and treat this craft individually.

This boat offers no difficulty in lofting, but may be built by laying down the body plan only. As repeated elsewhere, there is much in favor of completely lofting any boat. The assembly and type of frame are as shown in Fig. No. 6. The floors are in one piece from side to side except where cut by centreboard trunk. Put cross-bands on frames Nos. 1, 3, 6, and 8 only, with top edge to set-up line, as in Fig. No. 6. Cut off floors of frames Nos. 4 and 5, one and one-eighth inches from centreline to allow for trunk. Fasten frame together with $1\frac{1}{2}$" No. 10 screws. Transom offsets are to the tilted transom and not to station No. 10, and in case you loft half-breadth and profile lines use dimensions on these plans. Do not cut stem side bevel above sheerline, as it must show square above the deck.

Fig. No. 9 shows set up of a similar boat; the outer edges

of erecting stringers should be nineteen inches from centreline, as on body plan. Set up transom, the frames with cross-bands, and the stem, and run one ribband each side just below sheerline and one on bottom, where shown in the sketch.

The centreboard trunk should now be built; place together the boards for one side and lay out the radius shown and place the 3/4″ × 3″ oak head pieces accordingly. The over-all length of trunk must be at least four feet six inches to provide a little overlength for fitting at frames. Place thick paint and a thin thread of cotton between joints and fasten to head pieces with 1½″ No. 10 screws. Two dowels are shown in fore and aft joint, and these may be about 3/8″ diameter, wood or large galvanized nails, cut to about 1½″ long. The for'd head piece should project about six inches above trunk in order to receive fastenings through the beam above. The 3/4″ × 4″ cheek pieces should be screw-fastened on each side, as shown, also the 1/2″ × 3″ stiffeners. The trunk may now be fitted and fastened in place; tack it to the cross-band on frame No. 3 and use 1¾″ No. 10 screws through the frame floors below. A brace or support may be necessary to the floor below.

The balance of the frames can now be fitted and Nos. 4 and 5 will notch into cheek pieces, as shown in midsection drawing. The chine pieces should be clamped on top of frames, marked and sawed to shape. Both edges may be sawed square and the outer one bevelled after fastening; use 1½″ No. 10 screws and put a butt block at joint, as shown.

Bottom planks are first, starting with the garboards, placing thick paint and cotton across transom and around centreboard slot. Screw-fasten to trunk and cheek pieces, using 1½″ No. 8 screws (see "Caulking"). Provide a 3/32″ caulking seam between planks and fasten to frames with 4d galvanized nails and to chine with 1″ screws or 1¼″ or 1½″ copper boat nails, clinched as for dory lap; use 6d nails in transom if of soft wood. The upper bilge plank is next (use 12″ plank); its top edge must be shaped so that it touches the second knuckle its full length; this will make the for'd and after ends each about two and one-half inches or three inches wide; a 1″ dory lap is now worked on this edge, as shown in midsection. The plank still holds its full width of 11½″ or 12″ at centre of boat, thus leaving insufficient width for the other bilge plank, so spring a batten along this edge, taking three inches off at centre of plank and nothing off at ends (see small detail). Work a 1″ dory lap along this edge also. Use this plank as a pattern for marking the shape of the top edge of the bottom bilge plank, so that the two laps will fit when planks are bent in

place. The upper plank is fastened first and then the lower one; put paint and cotton along edge of bottom plank (see "Caulking," also "Dory Lap"). There are no hard bends and steaming should not be necessary, but if plank seems stiff and brittle use hot water, as described under "Steaming Plank."

The side plank should offer little difficulty; the first or lower one will lap over the bilge plank, and on lines drawing is shown just how this lap changes from stem to frame No. 3; from here aft there is little change. Obtain shape of plank edge or spiling first, and then gauge in 1″ for the lap and with a small bevel and a chisel spot the bevels on plank at each frame and plane the lap fair between the spots. There will be little bevel aft of frame No. 3. Leave sheer strake until boat is turned over and clamp and beams are in.

Before turning boat plane a flat spot one and one-sixteenth inches wide on centreline, caulk and putty the seam and fit the keel or skeg. You will notice that it stops each side of centreboard slot and is continued each side by a 3/4″ oak strip; planking for'd should be flattened off for stem face before for'd piece is put on. Make this face about one and one-fourth inches wide. Where not too deep fasten keel to each frame with a large galvanized nail.

The keel battens should now be fitted between frames and well nailed into keel; their underside must be shaped or bevelled to fit planking. The clamp and deck beams are put in, as explained under that heading. There is a double beam at frame No. 3. The aft piece butts against trunk head piece on each side; fasten beams to frames with two 1½″ No. 10 screws. Cockpit stringers should be cut to the sheer of the boat; put in fillers and mast partner. Cut mast hole through partner and mortise in step. The spar rakes aft from perpendicular three inches in ten feet, use a straight edge and level or plumb bob. The sheer strake or top plank may now be put on, inside of boat painted, and the deck laid. Before putting on canvas and guards fit the stem face and fasten to stem with long screws.

Chain plates should go on before guards, and a good method of fastening them is into a 3/4″ × 3″ doubler on inside of planking, using 1½″ screws or, better still, brass flat-head bolts. The rudder braces are stock, although you may have to use a shoulder eye-bolt for the top gudgeon. Edge bolt rudder before tapering it. Spars, sails, and rigging are covered elsewhere in this book. See plans of *Flattee* for centreboard pin arrangement and description. The stem band is bent back over stem head, as shown, and the jib stay shackles to it.

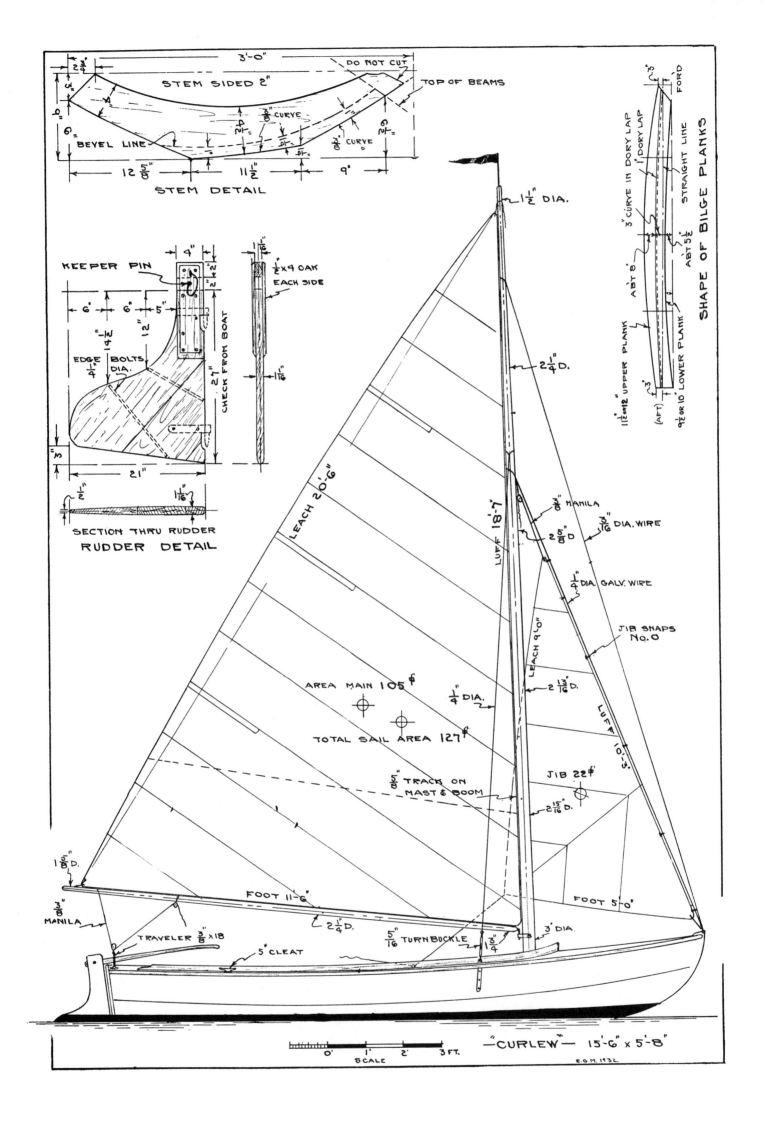

STEM DETAIL

STEM SIDED 2"
DO NOT CUT
TOP OF BEAMS
3'-0"
CURVE
BEVEL LINE
CURVE
12¼"
11½"
9"

SHAPE OF BILGE PLANKS
FORD
STRAIGHT LINE
3" CURVE IN DORY LAP
1" DORY LAP
ABT 8'
ABT 5½'
UPPER PLANK
LOWER PLANK
(AFT)

KEEPER PIN
½ X 4 OAK
EACH SIDE
CHECK FROM BOAT
EDGE
BOLTS DIA.
6"
6"
5"
27"
3"
21"

SECTION THRU RUDDER
RUDDER DETAIL

1½" DIA.
2¼" D.
LUFF 18'-7"
LEACH 20'-6"
⅝" MANILA
3/16" DIA. WIRE
¼" DIA. GALV. WIRE
2⅝" D
LEACH 9'-0"
JIB SNAPS No. 0
AREA MAIN 105 ф
TOTAL SAIL AREA 127 ф
¼" DIA.
2 13/16" D.
LUFF 10'-3"
⅝" TRACK ON MAST & BOOM
2 15/16" D.
JIB 22 ф
1⅝" D.
⅜" MANILA
FOOT 11'-6"
FOOT 5'-0"
2¼" D.
5/16" TURNBUCKLE
1¾"
3" DIA.
TRAVELER ⅜ X 18
5" CLEAT

"CURLEW" — 15'-6" x 5'-8"

0'   1'   2'   3 FT.
SCALE

E.G.M. 1932.

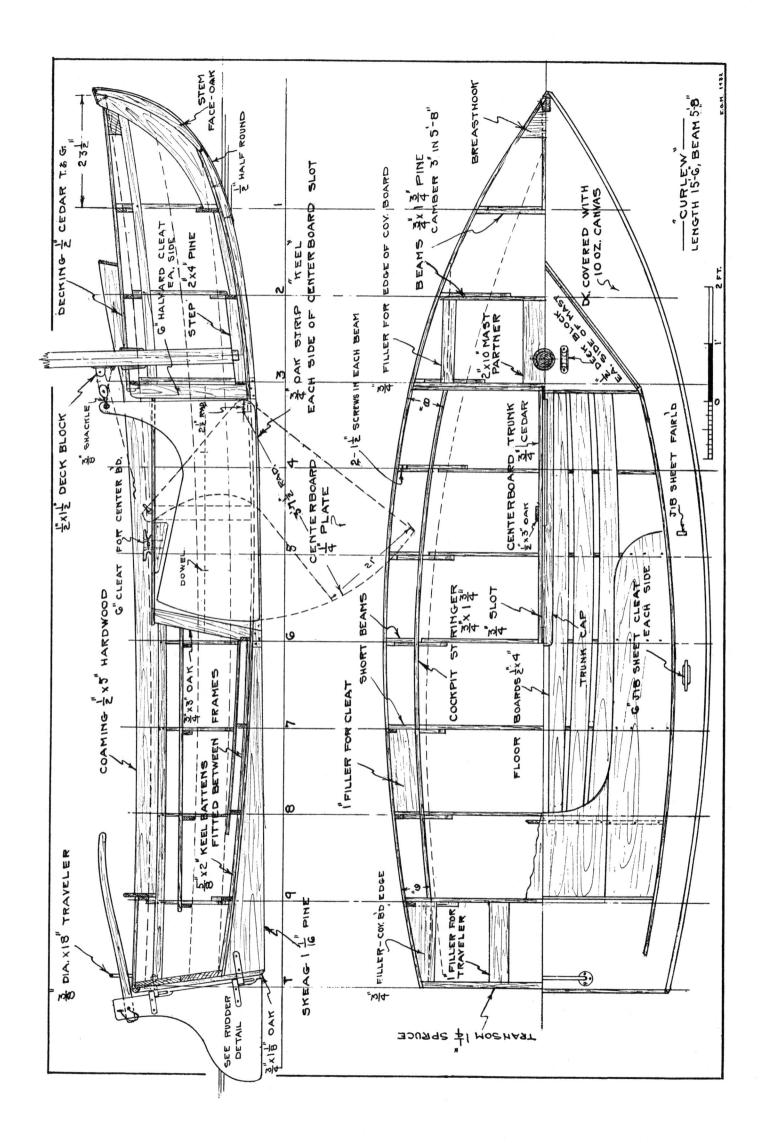

"CURLEW" — LENGTH 15'-6, BEAM 5'-8"

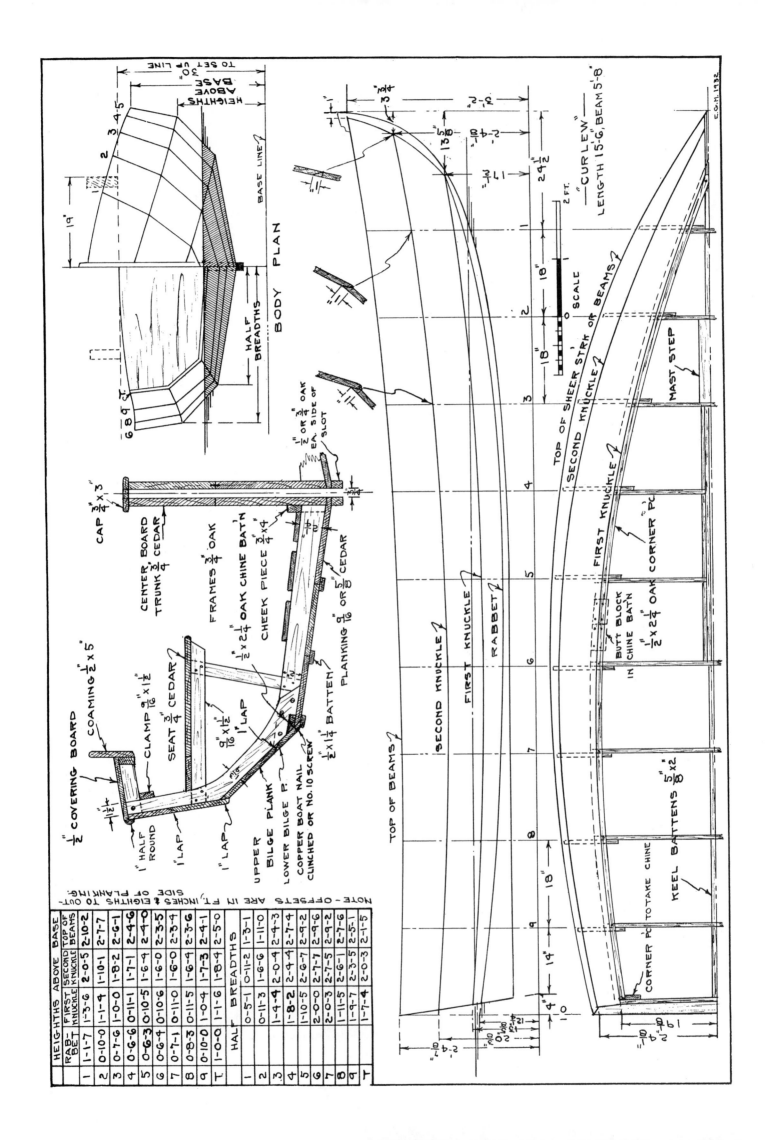

"CURLEW"
LENGTH 15'-6", BEAM 5'-8"

Ted Geary's "Flattee"

THIS BOAT WAS designed by "Ted" Geary the well-known yacht designer and racing skipper, and is published with his generous permission. Designed in 1928 as a class racer for the young sailors, it has met with wide approval and a large number have been built, most of them by their owners. The boat in the illustration is one of these and was built and very successfully raced by Norman Blanchard, Jr., of Seattle. A good "action" picture of the *Flattee* may be seen under *Truant*, a similar though smaller boat. They are exceptionally fast and at the same time quite safe enough, as the narrow cockpit and wide side deck make them almost non-sinkable. Like any boat of this type, they are capsizable, but float quite high and are easily righted again.

The construction is simplicity itself and no harder than the well-known skiff. The bottom is planked athwartship and, except for sides and backbone, most of the lumber may be of short lengths easily obtained and inexpensive.

When considering plans for a sailboat the advantages of building within a recognized class should be kept in mind. Class racing furnishes the only fair means of true competition in which you might say all men are equal. Local and intersectional races are arranged for desirable trophies, and the opportunities for advancement in the sport are limitless. All of the nationally known six- and eight-meter and R-Boat skippers started in just such craft as these, graduating later to the larger boats.

The Lumber Order

Backbone—2 pcs. ¾" × 10"—18' pine.
Side Plank—2 pcs. ⅝" × 16"—19' or 2 pcs. ⅝" × 10" and 2 pcs. ⅝" × 8".

Stem—1 pc. 1½" × 4"—16".
Transom—1 pc. ¾" × 14"—4' 2".
Centreboard and Rudder Trunks—2 pcs. ¾" × 10"—8'
Header Pieces—1 pc. ¾" × 3½"—4' and 1 pc. ¾" × 2" N.—3'.
Cheek Pieces and Stiffeners—2 pcs. ¾" × 4"—5' and 4 pcs. ½" × 3"—16".
Chine and Bottom Battens—2 pcs. ¾" × 2"—19' and 2 pcs. 18' and 2 pcs. 16'.
Frames—50 lineal feet ¾" × 2".
Bottom Plank—110 B. M. ⅝" × 7½" cedar, 4 and 5 feet lengths.
Deck Beams—3 pcs. ¾" × 12"—5'.
Cockpit Stringers—1 pc. ¾" × 6"—6'.
Mast Partner and Breasthook—1 pc. 2" × 12"—3'.
Deck—100 B. M. ½" × 3" T. and G.
Cockpit and Trunk Trim—1 pc. ½" × 8"—10'.
Guard—2 pcs. 1" halfround 19'.
Spars—1 pc. 3" × 3"—24', 1 pc. 2" × 2"—12' spruce.

The construction methods and details in the text of this book will apply closely here, and the following is intended to fill in the gaps and treat this craft individually.

This boat does not require lofting, except that stations Nos. 1, 2, and 4 and transom must be laid out to the dimensions and the forms assembled and transom cut out. Mark on each side of the centreline and cut the 2¼" slot for backbone, also cut the notches shown in forms for the chine pieces. The backbone is in two pieces, separated by the stern post, rudder, and centreboard headers, all ¾" thick, and at for'd end by the stem, which is 1½". The trunks must be watertight, so put thick paint and a thin thread of cotton between headers and side pieces. Treat the fore and aft seam between trunk edges and backbone in same manner, or, if lumber is quite dry, glue this joint. The ½″ × 3″ stiffeners are screw-fastened to each side, using 1″ No. 8 screws, and the backbone and trunk pieces are screw-fastened into the headers, using 1½″ No. 10 screws, or, better yet, ¼″ carriage bolts 2½″ long. To make sure that backbone will be straight fore and aft it should be tacked or fastened together on a straight surface such as floor or bench, slipping the stem in last. You will note that rudder stock is same diameter as width of slot, so plane about one-sixteenth off backbone between the rudder trunk headers before assembling. Also paint inside of rudder and centreboard trunks at same time. The frame stations are marked on outside of backbone and it will be close enough to square them down on each side of backbone from its top edge. As the forms must be fastened to backbone, fasten on each side at stations Nos. 1, 2, and 4 a ¾″ × 2″ or 3″ cleat on aft side of mark and allow it to stick up above backbone about 10″ to secure top edge of forms.

The transom is next screw-fastened to stern post, and square it athwartships from backbone pieces and brace to the latter. The forms are fastened in place to the cleats and should be so turned that the for'd edges of the side pieces are in line with the station mark, just as are the frames in the plan. Run a light ribband along each side on top of cross-bands and transom and square up each form. The whole should now be turned bottom up and tacked to horses and blocking ready for planking, much as in Fig. No. 9; see that there is no twist or wind in the boat. The chine pieces are next and the for'd ends must be bevelled to fit against sides of backbone at stem. The aft end will butt against transom and fasten to transom frame; nail into forms, and later when forms are removed the projecting nails may be cut off. Bevel edge of chine to conform with bottoms of transom and forms.

The two side planks are cut roughly to shape and the dimensions shown are purposely a half inch large, so a 15½″ plank can be made to do the trick. If such widths are not available, order the four narrower planks and make use of the dory lap as described in the text. I would paint the face of chines with marine glue, and fastening each plank at stem pull aft ends together with a rope, as described in the construction of *Truant*. Tack into forms only where necessary and screw-fasten to stem and transom with 1½″ No. 10 screws, placing a thin thread of cotton and thick paint between. Fasten into chine piece with copper boat nails clinched, or 1¼″ No. 8 screws; space fastenings about four inches and fasten before glue dries.

Notch out of the forms for the ¾″ × 1¾″ bottom battens shown in midsection, fit and fasten for'd ends against chines and butt against transom. The side plank edges should be planed fair and the bottom put on. As previously stated, it is planked athwartship. Provide a ³⁄₃₂″ caulking seam and place thick paint and a thin thread of cotton around trunks, transom, and side plank edges. Fasten with 6d galvanized nails and use 1½″ No. 8 screws around trunk edges. Fasten into the bottom battens as

each plank is put on, using 1½″ copper boat nails or 4d galvanized wire nails clinched inside. The for'd ends of side planks should be flattened off to form a 1½″ face and the stem face piece fastened; leave a ¾″ face on it for the jib stay chain plate.

Turning the boat over, the sheerline should be faired up and the frames may now be fitted against the sideboards; there are no bottom frames. Each one must be bevelled so that beams will fit flat against them later; the inside edges can remain square in this case. Fasten through plank into frame with 4d galvanized nails and at bottom of frame drill for and drive a 6d nail into chine; use a hold-on when driving nails.

The forms are left undisturbed until intermediate beams and frames are in place and then they are removed and the frame and beam put in their place. Fasten end of beams to each frame with two 1½″ No. 8 screws. The mast partner and breasthook and cleat fillers are fitted and before deck is laid the mast hole and step should be cut. Cut the 1½″ × 2″ mast step slot through the backbone pieces as shown and slip a ¾″ filler between them, fasten the ¾″ × 3½″ side pieces on each side; a ¼″ × 4½″ bolt at each end will be the best fastening. Cut the hole in the partner, lining it up with a straight edge set at the specified rake off backbone. There are four of the ¾″ × 1½″ deck braces shown in midsection, two on each side.

The whole interior should be painted and the deck laid, fastening to beams with 4d galvanized nails. The deck is then canvased and guards and trim put on. The trunk cap may be slotted full length of the trunk or just far enough to allow the arm to swing.

Centreboard and rudder will have to be made at a boiler or tank shop. Make a pattern of the angle of for'd end of centreboard. It should be such that when board is swung up its bottom edge will be flush with bottom of boat. By swinging it to the down position the length of arm can also be ascertained, checking length of centreboard to make sure it will house in the trunk. A ¼″ plate washer is welded or riveted to each side of the centreboard with a ¹⁷⁄₃₂″ or a ⁹⁄₁₆″ hole through for the pin as shown in detail. This makes the board ¾″ thick at this point; so that if the bolt is "hove up" too tightly it will not spring in the trunk sides and cause a leak. The hole for the pin through the backbone should be bored before backbone is set up. Measure up two and one-half inches from bottom edge of backbone and three and one-half inches aft of header at this height, and bore a half-inch hole at this point through cheek pieces and trunk.

The rudder is held in place by the keeper as shown; so installed, it is easily pulled up, leaving the bottom clear for beaching. The rudder is dropped into the slot, followed by the ¾″ wood keeper, which is prevented from dropping through by the ½″ × 1½″ cap shown in detail. The wedge is then shoved in aft of the keeper and the ¼″ diameter pin prevents it dropping down too far and jamming the rudder. The rudder rides on the washer shown.

The sheave arrangement on centreboard arm is a bit neater than shackle and block, though the latter is commonly used.

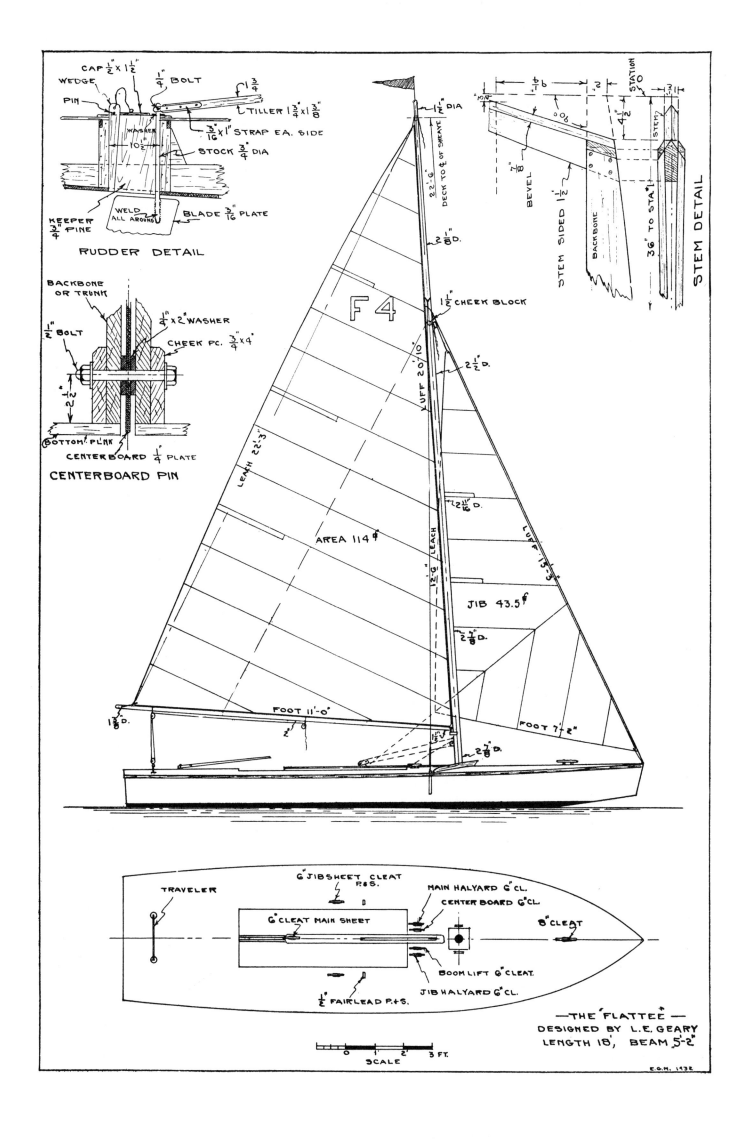

RUDDER DETAIL

CAP ½" × 1½"
WEDGE
PIN
¼" BOLT
Tiller 1¾" × 1⅜"
WASHER
3/16" × 1" STRAP EA. SIDE
STOCK ¾" DIA
KEEPER ¾" PINE
WELD ALL AROUND
BLADE 3/16" PLATE

CENTERBOARD PIN

BACKBONE OR TRUNK
½" BOLT
¼" × 2" WASHER
CHEEK PC. ¾" × 4"
BOTTOM PLANK
CENTERBOARD ¼" PLATE

STEM DETAIL

STEM SIDED 1½"
BEVEL ⅞"
BACKBONE
STATION 0
4½"
STEM
36" TO STA.1

F 4

1¾" DIA
22'-6" DECK TO ℄ OF SHEAVE
2⅛" D.
1½" CHEEK BLOCK
LUFF 20'-10"
2½" D.
2 11/16" D.
LEACH 22'-3"
AREA 114 ☐'
12'-6" LEACH
LUFF 15'-3"
JIB 43.5 ☐'
2⅛" D.
FOOT 11'-0"
1¾" D.
FOOT 7'-2"
2⅛" D.
2⅛" D.

TRAVELER
6" JIBSHEET CLEAT P.&S.
MAIN HALYARD 6" CL.
CENTER BOARD 6" CL.
6" CLEAT MAIN SHEET
8" CLEAT
BOOM LIFT 6" CLEAT.
JIB HALYARD 6" CL.
½" FAIRLEAD P.+S.

0   1   2   3 FT.
SCALE

—THE "FLATTEE"—
DESIGNED BY L.E. GEARY
LENGTH 18', BEAM 5'-2"

E.G.M. 1932

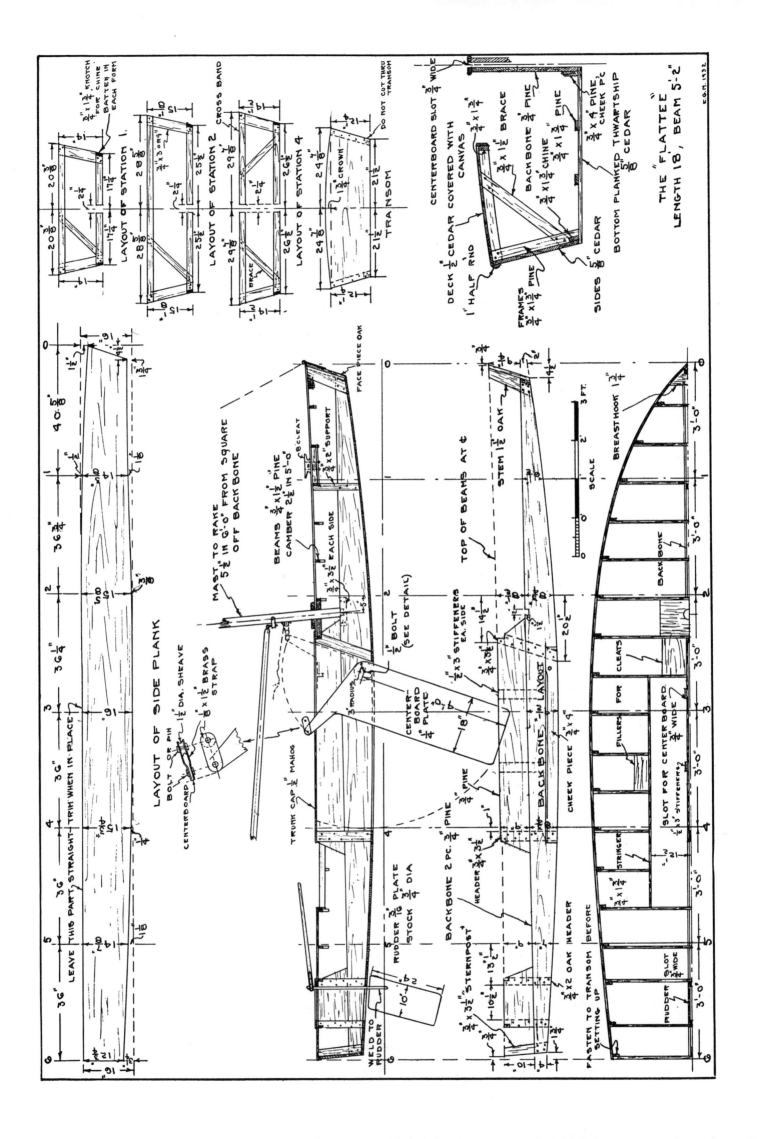

THE "FLATTEE"
LENGTH 18', BEAM 5'-2"

E.G.M. 1932

"Vagabond,"
A Keel Sloop

THE LIGHT FLAT-BOTTOMED centreboarder is all very well in its place and three such designs are shown in this book, but for a real tough boat it cannot compare with the keel sloop. This little boat is a pocket edition of a design from the boards of "Ted" Geary, with whom the author is associated. Three of these larger boats have been built—all very successful. One is owned and ably sailed by "Rudy" Pier of the Seattle Yacht Club. *Vagabond* was designed primarily as a cruiser, with limited accommodations for two, or as a safe little boat for afternoon sailing.

It is seventeen feet three inches long with a beam of six feet two inches, contains two berths and ample locker space. The small self-bailing cockpit with bridge deck at for'd end and the tightly closed companionway make for a safe little boat. Ballast consists of 866 pounds of cast iron, lead, or cement and boiler punchings, all outside. The displacement to designed load line is 2,760 pounds, and at this draft it will take 300 pounds to put the boat one inch deeper in the water. The hull shape combines the advantages of the round-bottom boat with the simplicity of construction found in the vee bottom. This shape has been incorporated in several of the author's published designs, the first being an eleven-foot sailing dinghy in a 1928 issue of *Motorboating*.

The rig has the modern jib-headed mainsail with track on mast and boom. The sail area is generous and for a heavy-weather country might be cut down a bit.

The Lumber Order

Keel and Deadwood—1 pc. 5½" × 9½"—12', 1 pc. 5½" × 9½"—6', all S. 4 S.
Sternpost—1 pc. 2½" × 6"—6' 6".
Stem—1 pc. 3½" × 12"—6'.
Anchor Stock—1 pc. 4½" × 8"—4'.
Sawed Frames—40 B. M. 1" N. × 6" and wider, 5' long and up, hardwood.

Floors—1 pc. 2½" × 8"—10' and 1 pc. 1⅝" × 8"—8'.
Transom—1 pc. 1¼" N. × 10"—12'.
Clamp—2 pcs. 1¼" × 2½"—18'.
Deck Beams and Headers—3 pcs. 1¹/₁₆" × 12"—6', 1 pc. 2½" × 12"—6'; 2 pcs. 2½" × 4"—4' (headers) and 1 pc. ⅞" × 12"—4' (trunk beams).
Corner Battens or Chines—4 pcs. ¾" × 2¾"—18' oak.
Deck Stiffeners—2 pcs. 1" × 4"—8'.
Mast Partner and Breasthook—1 pc. 2½" × 10"—6'.
Side Plank—12 pcs. ¾" × 6"—18'.
Bottom Plank—4 pcs. ¾" × 10"—16' and 2 pcs. ¾" × 12"—16'.
Bent Frames—25 pcs. ⅝" × ⅞"—5' and 20 pcs. 4' bending oak.
Cabin Trunk—2 pcs. ⅞" × 10"—10' and 1 pc. ⅞" × 12"—4'.
Main Deck, Cabin and Cockpit Floor—125 B. M. ¾" × 3" T. and G.
Trunk Deck—30 B. M. ½" × 3" T. and G.—vee joint one side.
Rudder—1 pc. 1½" × 8"—6' 6", 1 pc. 1" × 6"—3' 6" hardwood.
Tiller—1 pc. 1½" × 3"—4' hardwood.
Guards—2 pcs. 1¼" halfround 18'.
Bow Chocks—1 pc. 3" × 10"—6'.
Bulkheads—1 pc. 24" × 72" and 1 pc. 24" × 48"—½" plywood.
Mast—1 pc. 3½" × 3½"—27' spruce; *Boom*—1 pc. 2½" × 2½"—13' spruce.
Toe Rail—2 pcs. ⅞" × 1"—12'.

A few extra bent oak frames are included for breakage.

The construction methods and details in the text of this book will apply closely here, and the following is intended to fill in the gaps and treat this craft individually.

It is necessary to loft keel and stem profile or side view as well as the body plan, and, of course, it is really best to

83

completely lay down the entire lines of the boat. In doing so the transom may be a bit puzzling, but if you will refer from "shape of transom" detail to the half-breadth plan you will note how its dimensions were obtained and just enlarge this process on the floor. The lines for'd should fair into the ½" stem face half-siding from station No. 1 for'd, and here the rabbet and bearding lines will be obtained from the knuckle and sheer lines, just as they are from waterlines, etc., and in Fig. No. 1.

Wood patterns must be made in this case of keel, stem, sternpost, etc., and rabbet, bearding line, etc., marked. If lead or cast-iron keel is used a pattern must be made and bolts located and marked by what is known as core prints. These will represent the actual bolt protruding from the casting, about ½" on top and bottom, and mark in the moulding sand an impression for the moulder's core. Pine deck plugs will make suitable core prints and are just tacked in place. The core is made by the moulder and represents the bolt hole. The bolt head must also be taken care of so that it will be flush with bottom. The foundry will do this, if you explain what is wanted. If lead is used it should be in volume 1.22 square feet instead of 1.96 square feet, as for cast iron. Reduce depth of pattern to suit, also in both cases allow for shrinkage of the metal; when cooling cast iron shrinks one-eighth inch, and lead three-sixteenths inch per foot.

An inexpensive keel may be made from boiler punchings, cement, and sand. Leave top of form open and fasten $^{13}/_{16}$" dowels in it to represent bolts; put a piece on bottom end for bolt head. When pouring, reinforce the casting with at least four fore-and-aft rods $^{3}/_{8}$" or larger, and a large number of lighter rods or heavy wire athwartship. Slip an old saw down sides between concrete and form; also rap form with hammer to obtain a smooth outer surface. Boiler punchings weigh roughly 350 pounds per cubic foot, and should be mixed with enough sand and cement to bind the whole together, probably about one of cement, one of sand, and five parts of punchings, depending on size of the latter. The mould should contain about 2.7 cubic feet. When concrete has hardened the dowels may be driven out; to facilitate this, grease them well before the mixture is poured. The damp concrete is apt to swell the wood and necessitate boring out the dowel.

The frame is assembled much as in Fig. No. 5. Note that floor on frame No. 3 is on for'd side of frame; also on frame No. 6 put gussets on aft side, and on frame No. 2 on the for'd side in order to clear bulkheads. If cross-bands are kept five inches below sheer mark they will clear the clamp later. Frames Nos. 1, 2, 3, and 8 straddle keel as in detail of the runabout *Sunray*. The transom is assembled and screw-fastened from aft face into the cleats shown. If lumber is very dry, glue the joints; otherwise allow a seam for caulking.

The keel, sternpost, stem, etc., may all be fitted and bolted together before setting up. The keel casting is then clamped in place and holes for keel bolts drilled through the wood; put in and set up the for'd and aft bolt. The latter will have to be removed later; copper paint between all timbers if boat is for salt-water use.

Erect the boat as in Fig. No. 10 and allow room under keel to bore through floors and to drive keel bolts, either by removing a floor board or digging a hole, as the case may be. Place a shore under stem just for'd of station No. 1. Fasten transom to sternpost with 2½" No. 12 screws, as well as bolts shown. Run one ribband each side on topsides, keeping it clear of clamp fastening later, and one on bottom, well out. The bolt holes are now extended through the floors and the bolts put in; galvanized carriage bolts will do instead of the machine bolts shown. If you are cramped for space slide out keel. Extend holes through floors, insert bolts in keel casting, slide it in again, and drive the bolts.

The clamp, beams, and breasthook are next and the clamp may be tapered to ¾" at stem, and as a steam box will be needed for frames it might as well be made use of here and for planking. Where beams cannot be bolted to frames, bolt to clamp with a ¼" carriage bolt, and the three heavy beams should be bolted to both. The bulkheads can be most easily installed now, before boat is planked.

The shape of this boat makes planking particularly easy, as there is little edge set and no hard bends. The corner battens are fitted first and screw-fastened to each frame with two 1¾" No. 10 screws. On the body plan is shown the aft ends of planking about as they should be. You will note the narrow nib ends of strakes adjacent to chines; these are to eliminate edge set. The garboard should carry most of its width from midships aft to transom, and the for'd end will run out not far from station No. 2. The next plank is similarly laid out and the outside plank will then run full length of chine, with rather narrow ends. Fasten plank to frames with 1¾" galvanized boat nails. Make outer plank a little large and trim off with rabbet plane after fastening; use a template and trim a spot at each frame and plane between spots (see details). Start again with first bilge plank and same with the topsides. Put thick paint or glue on chine battens and fasten with 1½" copper boat nails, countersunk on outside and clinched over batten as for dory lap; space them about three inches apart. Properly done, this will make a watertight job without much dependence on caulking, which must be light at chine seam. Chine corners should be rounded off before caulking.

Obtain a thin batten, the same width as bent frames, and on inside of boat mark each side of each frame from keel to sheer. Drill through plank for fastenings, two in narrow and three in wide planks, and on outside counterbore for nail heads if it is found that they will not set into wood sufficiently for puttying. The frames are placed in steam box and one man inside will have to fit and fasten the hot frame to keel and fasten to chines and another outside drive plank fastenings. These should be 1½" copper boat nails (cut) driven against a hold-on, as in Fig. No. 18. Fasten heel to keel where possible and to chine battens with 3d galvanized wire nails. If all fastenings are driven while frame is hot it will not split.

The cockpit should now be tackled. The for'd beam is hung from the main deck beam above by the cockpit panelling or staving and does not extend to sides of boat, nor do any cockpit beams except at frame No. 8. The 1$^{1}/_{16}$" × 2" stringers extend from transom to for'd beam, and the intermediate beams are hung from it.

The cockpit may be scuppered out each side, but I have shown the floor slightly cupped toward the centreline and a single scupper run out through the stern above the waterline. This should be a ¾″ inside diameter lead pipe with ⅛″ walls. This may have its disadvantages, but is, I believe, safest; also the greater diameter of a single large scupper makes it less easily plugged and simpler to install. Cut holes in floor and hull for it, countersinking a one-half-inch margin all around to flush scupper flanges. Do this before cockpit floor is canvased. Later shove scupper through from aft and flange it over the canvas, using thick paint under flanges. Use a hardwood round stick and peen hammer to work the lead gradually into shape and fasten with copper boat nails.

Lay the cockpit floor, and from frame No. 8 aft extend the floor out to sides of boat for locker bottom. Fit and tack sides and aft end in place but do not fasten, as they must be removed later to give access to coaming boats.

The for'd deck, trunk, etc., are handled much as described for *Mariner,* and two companion slide details are shown in the plans of that boat. The 1″ × 4″ deck stiffeners are fastened before deck is laid with two ¼″ carriage bolts in the filler at for'd end and one in each wide beam.

The rudder may be made of one wide piece; in any case edge-bolt it first and trim to about ¾″ thick at aft edge. The for'd edge must be bevelled or rounded to suit pintle straps and to allow rudder to swing to about forty degrees. The braces are stock, and the top one must have a lock nut under pintle to prevent unshipping, or else cut pintle off flush with bottom of gudgeon and fit a hardwood block in the hole below it and fasten well with brass screws; this is called a wood lock.

The doorway is closed with a slide which just drops into the slots on each side of door jamb. The interior finish, berths, etc., are left to the builder. Spar making and rigging are pretty well covered under these headings. Temporary backstays are shown dotted, and if they are used the shrouds may be moved forward. The toe rail should have two or three ⅜″ × 2″ scuppers cut through at low point of sheer.

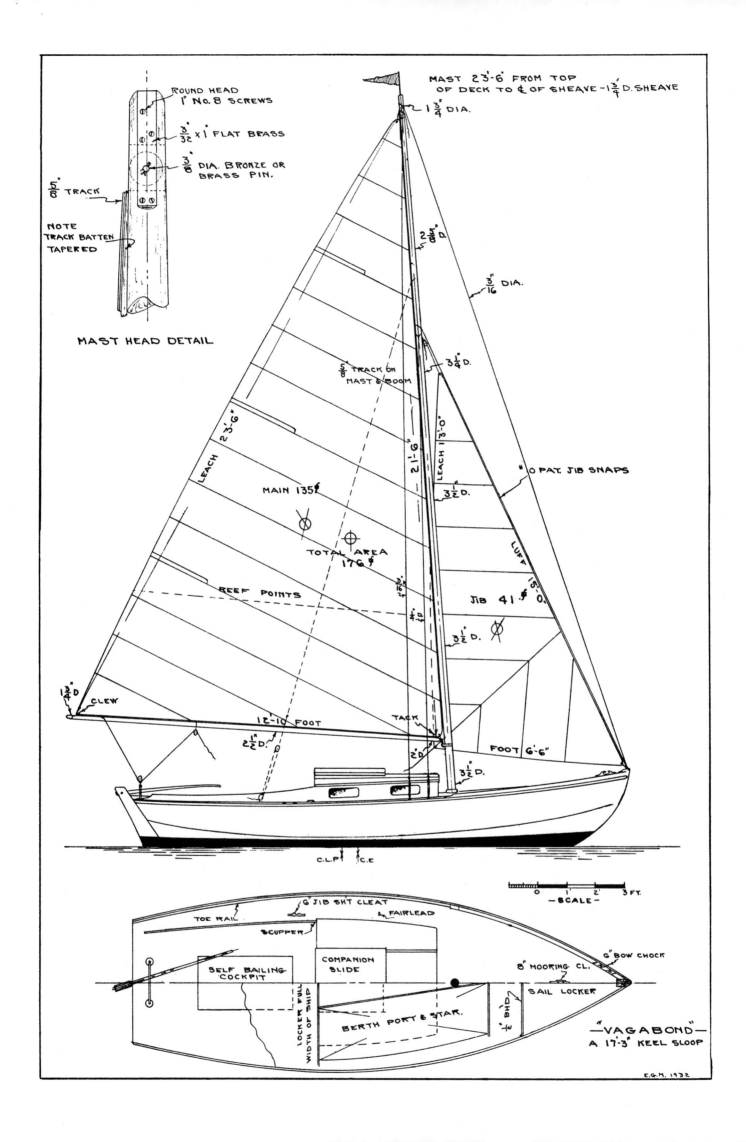

MAST HEAD DETAIL

ROUND HEAD
1" No.8 SCREWS

$\frac{3}{32}$" x 1" FLAT BRASS

$\frac{3}{8}$" DIA. BRONZE OR
BRASS PIN.

$\frac{5}{8}$" TRACK

NOTE
TRACK BATTEN
TAPERED

MAST 23'-6" FROM TOP
OF DECK TO ₵ OF SHEAVE - 1$\frac{3}{4}$" D. SHEAVE

1$\frac{3}{4}$" DIA.

2$\frac{1}{4}$" D.

$\frac{3}{16}$" DIA.

3$\frac{1}{4}$" D.

$\frac{5}{8}$" TRACK ON
MAST & BOOM

LEACH 13'-0"

"O PAT JIB SNAPS

3$\frac{1}{2}$" D.

LEACH 23'-6"

MAIN 135⁴

TOTAL AREA
176⁴

LUFF 15'-0"

JIB 41⁴

REEF POINTS

$\frac{3}{16}$" D.

4$\frac{1}{2}$" D.

3$\frac{1}{2}$" D.

1$\frac{3}{4}$" D.

CLEW

12'-10" FOOT

TACK

2$\frac{1}{2}$" D.

2" D.

FOOT 6'-6"

3$\frac{1}{2}$" D.

C.L.P.   C.E.

SCALE

0   1'   2'   3 FT.

TOE RAIL

6" JIB SHT CLEAT

4" FAIRLEAD

SCUPPER

SELF BAILING
COCKPIT

COMPANION
SLIDE

6" BOW CHOCK

8" MOORING CL.

SAIL LOCKER

LOCKER FULL
WIDTH OF SHIP

BERTH PORT & STAR.

$\frac{1}{2}$" BHD.

—VAGABOND—
A 17'-3" KEEL SLOOP

E.G.M. 1932

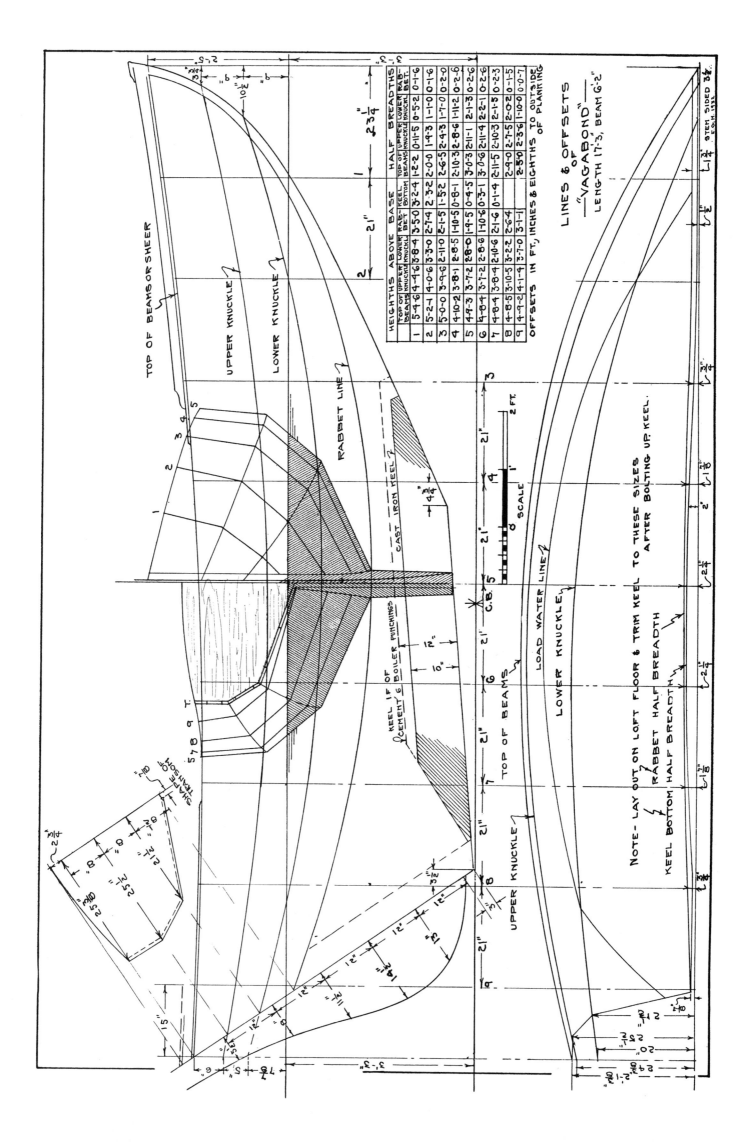

LINES & OFFSETS
of
"VAGABOND"
LENGTH 17'-3", BEAM 6'-2"

OFFSETS IN FT., INCHES & EIGHTHS TO OUTSIDE OF PLANKING

	HEIGHTS ABOVE BASE				HALF BREADTHS			
	TOP OF UPPER LOWER RAB-BEAMS KNUCKL KNUCKL		KEEL BET. BOTTOM		TOP OF UPPER LOWER RAB-BEAMS KNUCKLE KNUCKLE			BET.
1	5-4-6	4-6-3	3-5-0	3-2-4	1-2-2	0-11-5	0-5-2	0-1-6
2	5-2-1	4-0-6	3-3-0	2-7-4	2-0-0	1-4-3	1-1-0	0-1-6
3	5-0-0	3-9-6	2-11-0	2-1-5	2-6-5	2-4-3	1-7-0	0-2-0
4	4-10-2	3-8-1	2-8-5	1-10-5	2-10-3	2-8-6	1-11-2	0-2-6
5	4-9-3	3-7-2	2-8-0	1-9-5	3-0-3	2-11-1	2-1-3	0-2-6
6	4-8-4	3-7-2	2-8-6	1-10-6	3-0-6	2-11-4	2-2-1	0-2-6
7	4-8-4	3-8-4	2-10-6	2-1-6	2-10-3	2-11-5	2-1-5	0-2-3
8	4-8-5	3-10-5	3-2-2	2-6-4	2-4-0	2-7-5	2-0	0-1-5
9	4-9-2	4-1-4	3-7-0	3-1-1	2-5-0	2-3-6	1-10-0	0-0-7

TOP OF BEAMS OR SHEER

UPPER KNUCKLE

LOWER KNUCKLE

RABBET LINE

CAST IRON KEEL

KEEL IF OF CEMENT & BOILER PUNCHINGS

C.B.

TOP OF BEAMS

LOAD WATER LINE

LOWER KNUCKLE

UPPER KNUCKLE

SCALE

2 FT.

SHAPE OF TRANSOM

STEM SIDED 3¼

NOTE- LAY OUT ON LOFT FLOOR & TRIM KEEL TO THESE SIZES AFTER BOLTING UP KEEL.

RABBET HALF BREADTH

KEEL BOTTOM HALF BREADTH

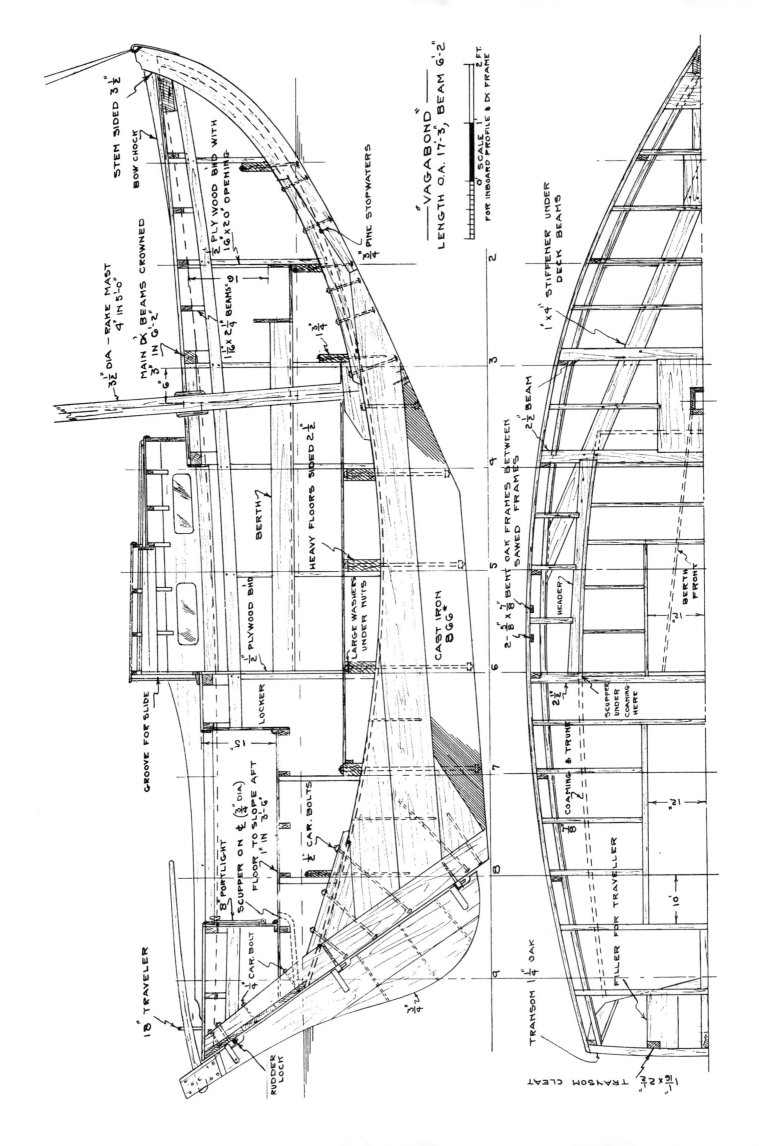

"VAGABOND"
LENGTH O.A. 17'-3", BEAM 6'-2"

0'   Scale   1'   2 FT.
FOR INBOARD PROFILE & DX FRAME

STEM SIDED 3½"

BOW CHOCK

3½" DIA — RAKE MAST 4" IN 5'-0"

MAIN DX BEAMS CROWNED

½ PLYWOOD BHD WITH 16"x20" OPENING

1 1/16 x 2¼" BEAMS — 9"

¾" PINE STOPWATERS

3" IN 6'-2"

6"

1¾"

GROOVE FOR SLIDE

BERTH

½" PLYWOOD BHD

HEAVY FLOORS SIDED 2½"

LARGE WASHERS UNDER NUTS

CAST IRON 866#

2 — ⅝ x ⅞" BENT OAK FRAMES BETWEEN SAWED FRAMES

1" x 4" STIFFENER UNDER DECK BEAMS

2½" BEAM

HEADER

BERTH FRONT

21"

18" TRAVELER

LOCKER

PORTLIGHT

8" PORTLIGHT

SCUPPER ON ℄ (¾" DIA)

FLOOR TO SLOPE AFT 1" IN 3'-6"

½" CAR. BOLTS

¼" CAR. BOLT

RUDDER LOCK

¼" CAR. BOLT

15"

2½"
2½"

SCUPPER UNDER COAMING HERE

COAMING & TRUNK ⅞"

21"

10'

TRANSOM 1¼" OAK

FILLER FOR TRAVELLER

3½"

¾"

1 1/16 x 2½" TRANSOM CLEAT

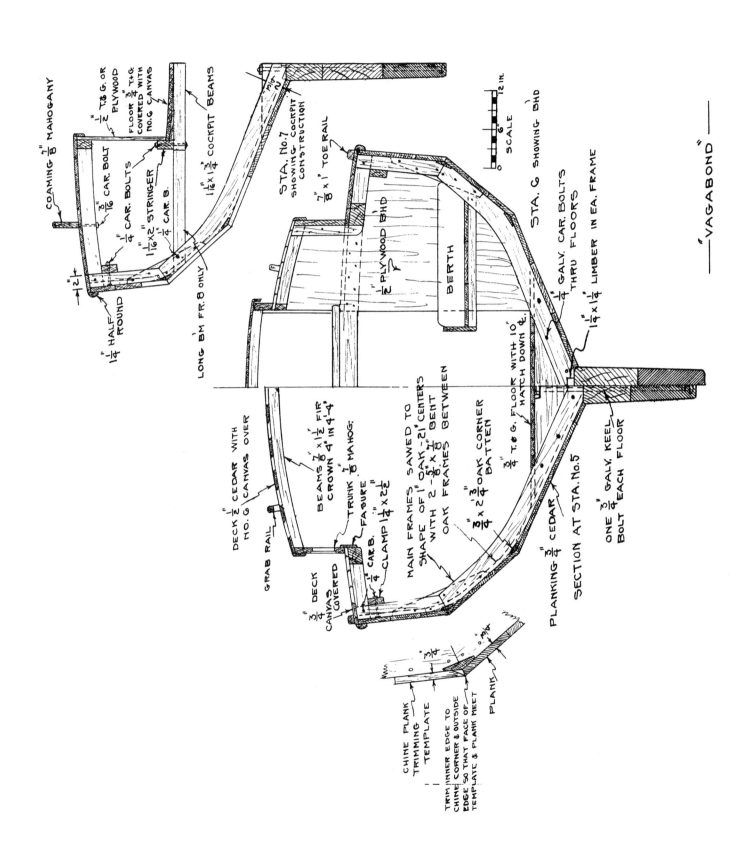

COAMING ⅞" MAHOGANY

½" T&G. OR PLYWOOD

FLOOR ¾" T&G. COVERED WITH NO. 6 CANVAS

¾₁₆ CAR. BOLT

¼" CAR. BOLTS

1⅟₁₆ x 2 STRINGER

¼" CAR. B.

1⅟₁₆ x 1¾ COCKPIT BEAMS

STA. No. 7
SHOWING COCKPIT CONSTRUCTION

⅞" x 1" TOE RAIL

LONG BM FR. 8 ONLY

1¼" HALF ROUND

½" PLYWOOD BHD

BERTH

STA. 6 SHOWING BHD

¼" GALV. CAR. BOLTS THRU FLOORS

1¼ x 1¼ LIMBER IN EA. FRAME

DECK ½" CEDAR WITH NO. 6 CANVAS OVER

GRAB RAIL

¾" DECK CANVAS COVERED

BEAMS ⅞" x 1½" FIR CROWN 4" IN 4'-4"

TRUNK ⅞" MAHOG.

¼" CAR. B.

CLAMP 1¼ x 2½

MAIN FRAMES SAWED TO SHAPE OF 1" OAK - 21" CENTERS WITH 2 - ⅝" x ⅞" BENT OAK FRAMES BETWEEN

¾ x 2¾ OAK CORNER BATTEN

¾" T.&G. FLOOR WITH 10" HATCH DOWN ℄

PLANKING ¾" CEDAR

SECTION AT STA. No. 5

ONE ⅜" GALV. KEEL BOLT EACH FLOOR

CHINE PLANK TRIMMING TEMPLATE

TRIM INNER EDGE TO CHINE CORNER & OUTSIDE EDGE SO THAT FACE OF TEMPLATE & PLANK MEET

¾"

PLANK

SCALE
12 IN.
6"
0

— "VAGABOND" —